·CAL

Limiting Population Growth
and the Ford Foundation Contribution

Department of Social and Administrative Studies,
Barnett House,
Wellington Square,
Oxford.

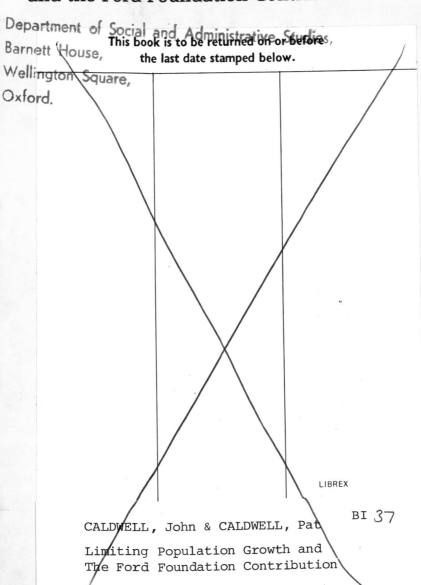

CALDWELL, John & CALDWELL, Pat

Limiting Population Growth and
The Ford Foundation Contribution

Limiting Population Growth
and
The Ford Foundation Contribution

John Caldwell and Pat Caldwell

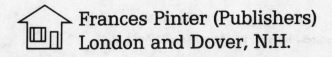

Frances Pinter (Publishers)
London and Dover, N.H.

© The Ford Foundation 1986

First published in Great Britain in 1986 by
Frances Pinter (Publishers) Limited
25 Floral Street, London WC2E 9DS

Published in the United States of America in 1986 by
Frances Pinter (Publishers) Limited
51, Washington Street
Dover, New Hampshire

Library of Congress Cataloging-in-Publication Data
Caldwell, John Charles.
    Limiting population growth and the Ford
Foundation contribution.

    1. Population assistance, American.
2. Ford Foundation.   I. Caldwell,
Patricia (Patricia Rosie Clara)   II. Title.
HB884.5.C35   1985   304.6'6'091724   85–16975
ISBN 0-86187-576-1

British Library Cataloguing in Publication Data
Caldwell, John C. (John Charles)
    Limiting population growth and the Ford Foundation
    contribution.
    1. Ford Foundation—History
    2. Population policy
    I. Title   II. Caldwell, Pat
    363.9'1   HB883.5

    ISBN 0-86187-576-1

Typeset by Joshua Associates Ltd, Oxford
Printed in Great Britain by Biddles of Guildford Ltd.

Contents

Preface

This book is largely based on work extending from August 1982 until September 1983 and draws upon studies of records held by the Ford Foundation and other institutions as well as upon numerous interviews conducted around the world between November 1982 and March 1983. In the Ford Foundation we wish to thank particularly Oscar Harkavy and, for his archival work, Tim Rice.

For its knowledge of the impact of population programs and of the mechanics of national policy change, the study also draws upon largely unpublished work undertaken by John and Pat Caldwell as a study of the origins of population policies between October 1968 and February 1969 in South Korea, Taiwan, Philippines, Hong Kong, Indonesia, Singapore, Malaysia, East Pakistan (Bangladesh), West (Pakistan (Pakistan), Iran, and Turkey, encouraged by Parker Mauldin when John Caldwell was Regional Demographic Director for Africa with the Population Council and from a period in Latin American in 1981 supported by the Ford Foundation. Over the last quarter of a century support for related work in the Third World has mostly come from the Australian National University and the Population Council and through attachments to ECAFE (now ESCAP); the Universities of Ghana, Ibadan, Ife, Nigeria (Nsukka), and Nairobi; The Cairo Demographic Centre; the International Diarrhoeal Diseases Centre, Bangladesh; and the Population Centre, Bangalore.

In the Department of Demography, Australian National University, assistance on this project has been received from Wendy Cosford, Pat Quiggin, Inge Kral, Daphne Broers-Freeman, and Kae Mardus.

The book is essentially a record of the situation up to

1983. It might be noted that at the end of 1984 Ronald Freedman wrote an evaluation of the Hewlett Foundation support for the Population Centers at American Universities concluding that this funding was sufficient to ensure the continuing health of the Centers and their contact with the Third World.

John and Pat Caldwell

The approach

The Ford Foundation has spent around $270 million on population activities ranging from biomedical research on human reproduction, which absorbed about half this expenditure, to demography (together with related social sciences) and assistance to family planning programs.[1] The Foundation entered the field in 1952 with a grant to the Population Reference Bureau, followed, in 1954, by its first support for the Population Council.

Within the larger context, this book will focus on the $45 million investment in the development of graduate education in the population field within the areas of the social sciences and public health from 1960, both in the United States and beyond. Ford Foundation funding was the major element in developing large integrated population programs with a substantial concern with the Third World. For almost a decade it could have been said, in a funding sense, to have dominated the field, until American Government expenditure began to grow massively. This book will explore why this happened and what it appears to have achieved.

We feel that it is important to place the Ford Foundation intervention into an adequate historical context. Why did it enter the population field? Why did no major foundation do so earlier? How had population research and teaching previously developed without such support and why was it sufficiently strong in the 1960s to be able to absorb the funding that so suddenly became available? What was the aim and what was the achievement? What is the future both for the Ford Foundation in this context and for the population field?

It may be worthwhile to look ahead and underscore a few salient points. The first is that the scale of the Ford intervention into population education was an act of will rather than a reluctant concession to persistent pressure. In the surviving mountain of public and confidential documents from the immediately preceding period there is mention of the need for a specialized teaching program in the United States, but no suggestion that the Ford Foundation or others might move to the almost simultaneous establishment of a dozen programs in the United States and of half that number abroad.

The second is that the Ford program worked actively toward its own diminution in that Ford officers played a significant role in bringing the Government into population education so that the unique Ford contribution spanned less than a decade. However, it is pertinent to enquire as to whether this was a critical period or merely a decade saved and also as to whether the Ford Foundation intervention created a qualitatively different form of population studies than Government intervention alone would have achieved.

The third is the underlying purpose of the Ford Foundation move and its degree of success. Undoubtedly, the major purpose was to play a role in the attempt to slow down world population growth. There are now signs that total growth may not be as great as was once feared. The United Nations 'medium' world population projection for the year 2000 peaked with the 1968 projections at 6.4 billions and had by the 1980 projections fallen to 6.1 billions. Even this change does not tell the whole story. When the Foundation entered the population field there was apprehension that events would continue to outrun prediction. The 1958 medium projection for the 1980 population was 600 million people (or 16 per cent) above the 1954 projection and one billion (or 19 per cent) above the 1950 projection.[2] Many observers felt that the future had been contained, or at least our ability to reduce mortality had been finally understood, when the projections plateaued after 1958 and peaked in 1973. It is clear that the success of national family planning programs and considerable social change have played a role in reducing the likely ceiling to world population growth. In 1974 we put the probable ceiling at from 11 billions in 2050 to 15 billions in 2100, depending on the degree of intervention and change,[3] while recent United Nations estimates now suggest a range from about 9.6 billions in 2050 to 9.9 billions in 2100.[4] Clearly, confidence is growing that the world can achieve a near stationary population that it can provide with an acceptable standard of living. A pertinent question is whether planned intervention has played a part in curbing numbers and whether the Ford Foundation assisted significantly in this process. First, we must explain how Ford's intervention was possible at all.

The establishment of the population field

Thomas Malthus was the father of demography to an extent that has not been the case with the major figures in many other fields. The proposition he put forward in 1798 in an *Essay on the Principle of Population*, namely that population tends to outrun the food supply with the result that high mortality constrains the growth rate, influenced the way that nearly every demographer viewed non-industrialized societies until the 1950s. Indeed, the Ford Foundation intervention can be viewed as an immediate result of the retreat of the Malthusian specter as fast population growth rates were established for an increasing number of Asian countries. Malthus was also important in this story in another way. The account of the West's interest (especially that of the British) in non-industrialized populations and of Ford Foundation interests both in population and other areas is peculiarly strongly related to India. An important reason is that Malthus was Professor of Political Economy in the East India Company's College at Haileybury from 1805, soon after its founding, until 1834, and he and his successors ensured that generations of British officials and scholars in India saw that country's society in Malthusian terms, as is evidenced by every Indian Census Report until 1951 (the one that was presented with great effectiveness to the 1954 World Population Conference in Rome).[5]

However, the most forceful impetus to the spread of demographic studies was the decline in Western fertility which began in France at the end of the eighteenth century and occurred in most of north-west and central Europe as well as English-speaking areas of overseas European settlement in the last three decades of the nineteenth century. By the first decades of the twentieth century there was sufficient secure population data for the development of theories about population growth and the world's future population. It is from this time that apprehension begins to develop about what these trends imply unless some kind of intervention should prove possible.

In 1917 George Knibbs collected population estimates from 1600 onward and employed nineteenth- and twentieth-century population figures to show what was happening to the world's population.[6] This brave attempt was the origin of two erroneous schools of thought which were not fully disproved until after the Second World War. First, because the figures were dominated by those from the developed world, he concluded 'the rate of increase in the earlier part of last century has fallen off and the world's population increase will continue at a less rapid rate.'[7] Subsequently, the publication in 1931 by W. R. Crocker of *The Japanese Population Problem: The Coming Crisis* permanently wrote the Japanese experience into demographic thinking.[8] In 1931 Willcox added to Knibbs's list of earlier population sources and also employed the three new periodic estimates of world population figures originating in the interwar years from the League of Nations, the International Institute of Agriculture and the International Statistical Institute.[9] Nevertheless, William Willcox, constructing a population curve too similar to that of Knibbs for safety, also concluded: 'This evidence indicates that in less than three centuries the population of the earth has nearly quadrupled and that the rate of its increase accelerated until about 1900 but slackened after that date.'[10] Second, Raymond Pearl, acknowledging Knibbs as his stimulus,[11] described his S-shaped logistic curve in 1924,[12] thereby implying the likelihood of a slackening in population growth.

Nevertheless, the origin of modern apprehensions about world growth potential lies in the development and application of component methods for projecting populations. Such projections had an immense impact in the 1950s and help to explain the timing of Ford Foundation and other interventions.[13] They date back to the early 1920s but received a powerful impetus in the United States from a paper published by Pascal Whelpton in 1928[14] and by population projections undertaken by him and Warren Thompson for the American Government in the early 1930s.[15]

The origins of much of the research of the 1960s and 1970s, especially the KAP studies[16] and the World Fertility Surveys,[17] traced back to the hesitant steps taken from the early stages of the fertility decline to explain how individual couples had controlled their fertility. There was early evidence that periodic or more permanent sexual abstinence played a role.[18] Nevertheless, government statisticians[19] and public enquiries[20] tended to assume that the major role was played by chemical or mechanical contraception. Coghlan wrote in 1903, 'in the years following 1880 the art of applying artificial checks to conception was successfully learnt and has continued in operation to this day. Nor are there any present signs that the lessons thus learnt are likely to be forgotten.'[21] However, it was the growth of the social sciences in the United States during the 1920s and the very low fertility levels achieved by the early 1930s that spurred investigators to cross-question those actually involved. By 1934, Frank Lorimer and Frederick Osborn were able to compare evidence on the type of contraceptive practice[22] from three sources: the 1929 study by the Lynds of Middletown,[23] the 1931–32 study of obstetrics hospital patients by Raymond Pearl[24] and a study by Regine Stix and Frank Notestein of clients during the same period who had attended family planning clinics in the Bronx.[25] None of these samples could be said to be representative of the United States. The findings did not agree and those of Stix and Notestein, which were of a population predominantly of European birth and Jewish religion, showed a very great reliance before attendance at the clinic on the employment of withdrawal or *coitus interruptus,*[26] greater than that indicated by Pearl. Nevertheless, Notestein was convinced that the evidence

showed that contraceptive technology was of little importance compared with social change and the desire to control
fertility. He was greatly impressed by Norman Himes's 1936
publication, *The Medical History of Contraception*,[27] which
claimed knowledge of fertility control methods throughout
much of human history and hence implied that they could
have been employed as soon as lower fertility was desired.
He regarded this viewpoint as having been confirmed by Lewis-
Faning's survey of hospital patients for the British Royal
Commission on the birth rate,[28] and it has remained one
element in the population debate, as is evidenced by Paul
Demeny's report on Bangladesh in the mid-1970s.[29] However,
the first contraceptive-use household survey was conducted
in Indianapolis in 1941[30] and this work was the direct
ancestor of the important Third World surveys of the postwar
period which played a central role in stimulating population
control efforts.

Nevertheless, the build-up of knowledge and experienced
persons should be seen in proper perspective. The Indianapolis
survey, like most of the preceding work, was dominated by
an interest in declining fertility, particularly in fertility
differentials. It was the differential rate of reproduction by
social class and supposedly related inherent characteristics of
intelligence and even character that had brought most of the
real professionals to the study of fertility. The Eugenics movement had held its First International Congress in London
as early as 1912[31] and provided a major force for the founding of journals, the holding of conferences and the funding of
research between the Wars. Notable figures who began their
intellectual journey in the movement included Julian Huxley,
Lionel Penrose and C. P. Blacker in England and in the
United States both Henry F. and Frederick Osborn, Robert
Cook and Raymond Pearl. They formed the strongest con-
tingent to the First International Population Conference
in 1927.[32] Furthermore, they established a precedent in
terms of population scientists becoming involved with
governmental attempts to control fertility. They advocated

the compulsory sterilization of the unfit, especially once the necessary operations had been perfected in the late 1890s. By 1935, 20,000 compulsory sterilizations had been performed in the United States, of which half were in California.[33] The interest of the Eugenics movement in differential birth rates was sustained by demographers into the 1960s partly because such measures were seen increasingly as evidence that fertility decline had begun in a section of the population, the interest ceasing with the advent of such methods as the pill, the IUD and sterilization, the use of which is much less related to socio-economic class.

Emerging more slowly was a persistent interest in population growth itself and in its underlying laws which might predict the future as well as explain the past. In 1916, Walter Willcox, who was later to teach Frank Notestein, concluded that fertility decline must inevitably follow mortality decline:

In considering this change [the falling birth-rate] may I first suggest that some such change was an almost necessary consequence of the great decline in the death-rate? . . . It is the decline in the birth rate, and only that, which has enabled mankind to grip and hold fast the advantages promised by the decline in the death rate.[34]

By the second half of the 1920s, voices began to be heard which claimed that world population growth was only too likely to force the population of the planet to press disastrously upon the means of subsistence. Indeed, it was to be the 1950s before the disadvantages of population growth were to be commonly measured by other yardsticks than the Malthusian preoccupation with food. The Announcement for the conference that Margaret Sanger organized in Geneva in 1927 read:

The World Population Conference represents a pioneer effort on an international scale to grapple with one of the most fundamental problems which mankind faces today.

The earth, and every geographical division of it, is strictly limited in size and in ability to support human populations. But these populations keep on growing; and in so doing they are creating social, economic and political situations which threaten to alter profoundly our present civilization, and perhaps ultimately to wreck it.[35]

Professor East of Harvard repeatedly emphasized the threat, claiming that every human being required two and a half acres of land for support.[36] The same year Edward Ross spelt out the same message in his *Standing Room Only?*[37]

The situation was examined more scientifically the following year by G. H. Knibbs in *The Shadow of the World's Future or the Earth's Population Possibilities and the Consequences of the Present Rate of Increase of the Earth's Inhabitants.*[38] Knibbs concluded that China's population had grown as fast between 1715 and 1835 as did the population of Europe between 1800 and 1920. He calculated that world population was already growing at 1 per cent per annum and that the earth's ultimate carrying capacity lay between 11 and 12 billions.

Some of the roots of the later interest in the mechanics of demographic transition lay in the work of A. M. Carr-Saunders. In 1922, in his book *The Population Problem,*[39] he discerned three stages of fertility control: a variety of institutional controls and birth control practices among primitive peoples, a transitional stage when these wither, and a final stage of modern fertility control. The descendants of these ideas included both Frank Notestein's cultural support for high fertility and the three stages of demographic change (which Notestein acknowledged), as well as recent interests both in traditional fertility control and in the rise of fertility in the early stages of demographic transition. Indeed, Edye, when reporting the 1921 Indian Census and discounting the impact of the influenza epidemic as aberrant, claimed that India had already entered the second phase and was growing rapidly.[40] In 1936, Carr-Saunders was able to document in his *World*

Population[41] massive population growth in Japan, Eastern Europe, India, Ceylon, Egypt, Algeria, Formosa and the Philippines. He argued that Third World populations were tending to increase but that the gains from mortality decline were unlikely to be retained unless fertility could also be controlled. On the latter point, he received encouragement from Hutton's 1931 Indian Census Report on the stirrings of the birth control movement in that country and argued that if fertility control could spread in India then it was culturally probable that it could do so in China and Java as well. The evidence for a very great potential for population growth in eastern and southern Europe had already been underlined in the second volume of the work of his colleague, R. R. Kuczynski, *The Balance of Births and Deaths*, commissioned by the Brookings Institute and published in 1931.[42]

Earlier than Brookings, two small American foundations had already begun to fund population work. The Scripps Foundation started in 1922 in Ohio and supported Warren Thompson and P. K. Whelpton, originally with the idea that much of their work would be in Asia. In 1928, the Milbank Memorial Fund opened a Population Research Office with Edgar Sydenstricker in charge, joined shortly afterwards by Frank Notestein and later by Clyde Kiser. The following year the Population Reference Bureau began its work. Meanwhile, the institutional structure of population studies was being established with the formation of the International Union for the Scientific Study of Population in 1928 and the Population Association of America in 1932. Both organizations published journals, while after 1936 when the Milbank Memorial Fund financed the establishment of the Office of Population Research at Princeton University, these were joined by *Population Literature*, which later became *Population Index*. Nevertheless, the most important series of population journal articles from 1928 until after the Second World War were those published in sections of the *Milbank Memorial Fund Quarterly*.

The early interest in Third World populations drew largely upon colonial censuses. However, in 1929, the Milbank Memorial Fund financed a survey in rural China carried out by John Lossing Buck which was reported in the *Milbank Memorial Fund Quarterly*,[43] where in 1938 Frank Notestein argued that the population of rural China around 1930 was already growing at 1.2 per cent per annum.[44] In 1927 and 1929, E. F. Penrose had reported to conferences of the Institute of Pacific Relations both substantial population growth in Japan and also declining fertility explained by spreading birth control. Later he wrote,

> It would seem that when a community has gained the knowledge and acquired the habits necessary to reduce the death-rate it will sooner or later gain the knowledge and acquire the habits necessary to reduce the birth-rate. There may be a time lag between the two processes, but both of them in a large sense are the outcome of education.[45]

By the late 1930s, Wendell Cleland, an American who had taught in Egypt since 1917 and had published in 1931 *The Population Problem in Egypt*,[46] was advocating the intervention of the Egyptian Government into the area of fertility control.[47]

Thus, by the end of the interwar years, there were visions of the population activities of future decades beginning to emerge. A key part of the story was what happened at the very end of that period and at the Office of Population Research, Princeton, during the Second World War.

> In January 1939 the Council of the League of Nations, in execution of a resolution adopted by the Assembly, appointed a committee to study demographic problems in their economic, financial and social setting, and to submit a report on the subject which might be of practical value to governments in the determination of their policies.[48]

This might well have come to nothing but for the shift of

the League's Economic, Financial, and Transport Department to Princeton where, in 1941, agreement was reached that work on European populations should begin in Princeton University's Office of Population Research funded by the Carnegie Corporation through the Milbank Memorial Fund. Ultimately, four books on Europe were produced.[49] These studies had by 1943 convinced Frank Notestein that the demographic transition of western Europe was being repeated in southern and eastern Europe as economic change spread there. In February 1943, he reported to the American Philosophical Society the essence of his later work:

> Unparalleled population growth . . . developed because of changes in birth and death rates so sweeping as to amount to a vital revolution. Before this vital revolution, high death rates nearly cancelled high birth rates to yield little natural increase. In the modern industrial West, where the revolution has most nearly run its course, both death and birth rates are now low, yielding again small increase. The rapid growth occurred during the period of transition from high to low vital rates because mortality led fertility in the downward trend. This entire pattern of lagging transition in vital rates, and the resulting wave of growth, did not begin simultaneously all over Europe. Instead it spread very slowly from West to East with the technical and industrial revolution. The result is that the various regions of Europe are in widely different phases of the wave of growth.[50]

The picture was expressed with an almost mathematical clarity that was immensely attractive. Notestein taught it each year in the Princeton course, adding more material and illustrations, until the end of the 1950s. This course was taken by most of the influential American demographers of the post-war era and by a majority of Third World students on Population Council Fellowships during the 1950s.

Nevertheless, the focus was still on the developed world. That changed in 1943, when, with war in the Pacific and emerging ideas of postwar reconstruction, the Geographer of the Department of State requested the Office of Population Research to undertake studies of two Asian countries. This was done with financial support from the Milbank Memorial Fund and the Rockefeller Foundation.[51] Following pre-war precepts, and also the availability of demographic data, India and Japan were chosen, resulting in two large books some years after the Second World War.[52] Ultimately, two further studies, one of Taiwan and the other of Malaya, were added.[53] The important point is that, as with the European project, the major impact on the demographers at the Office of Population Research occurred much earlier, when the earliest findings were being discussed and the first published results were coming out. As early as December 1943, Dudley Kirk was reporting to the American Sociological Society

In regard to demographic matters the different countries of the world may be considered as on a single continuum of development. . . . In a relatively stable postwar world these areas [the emphasis here extends mostly to Eastern and Southern Europe and to South America] will experience tremendous population growth, comparable in amount, though probably not in rate, to that experienced by the Western world at an earlier period in its history.[54]

Perhaps a clear turning point was the Milbank Memorial Fund's 22nd Annual Conference in early 1944, where the Round Table on Population Problems was presented with seven *Demographic Studies in Selected Areas of Rapid Growth.*[55] OPR research was presented on India, Japan and Egypt, and the participants reported unequivocally that the demographic transition was going to be a phenomenon of the whole world. Kingsley Davis, noting that the 1941 Indian Census had shown for the first time rapid population growth over two decades totalling 83 million, concluded: 'Thus at a time when the Western nations were approaching demographic stability, India, with its much larger population, was just starting what appears to be a period of rapid and gigantic expansion.' Kiser reported, 'In short, Egypt is in a demographic jam. With limited room for expansion and no early prospect for substantial decline in fertility, she faces mounting population pressure.' He commented on this occurring despite deplorable housing and sanitary conditions.

Yet the truth was that sanitary conditions had improved from a situation even more deplorable, and as a result death rates were falling and natural increase rising. This had been the message of each Indian Census Report since 1921 and Kingsley Davis had been convinced. Furthermore, it was now appreciated that death rates had fallen remarkably in both Taiwan and Korea as a result of Japanese colonization.[56] Davis reported that the 100 million people added to India's population since 1921 had been the result of British law and order, and famine control, of the improvement of transport, the extension of irrigation, the encouragement of a normal agricultural surplus for export, together with advanced famine warnings and famine relief, and the reduction of the great epidemic diseases, smallpox, cholera, plague and kala-azar.[57] This added an important new dimension to Notestein's theory of demographic transition. No longer was the Industrial Revolution needed to bring down death rates but only colonial and other Governments with the necessary strength, knowledge and efficiency. As early as his 1943 paper, Notestein had been arguing that in 'large regions in the Far East . . . a modicum of modern sanitation and police work has permitted a tremendous growth of peoples.'[58] At the 1944 Round Table he reported his belief that the application of existing medical techniques could produce growth in most of the non-industrialized world, noting that the annual rates of population growth in India had been 1.2 percent in 1921–41, in the Dutch East Indies 2.1 percent in 1920–30 and in the Philippines 2.2 percent in 1918–39. He argued that the eventual solution would involve basic social change but that one ingredient would have to be birth control facilities and widespread propaganda. Davis said that India needed better contraception and a sociologically intelligent program of fertility control. However, he also added another element to the OPR construct when he argued that colonialism made death control easier but fertility control harder because of the confrontation between colonial Governments and dependent people defending their own cultures.

This edifice was completed in a paper published by Notestein in 1945 in a book called *Food for the World*, edited by Theodore Schultz, which grew out of the Hotsprings Conference of 1943 and was a kind of offering for the proposed United Nations Food and Agriculture Organization.[59] He predicted that world population would be at least 3 billions by the year 2000, but, in keeping with Knibbs, Pearl, and Willcox, he showed the population growth of the world and each continent slackening after 1970, presumably as the result of greater pressure on resources. Nevertheless, every part of the world was promised a demographic transition (Notestein used this term for the first time but it was a phrase employed earlier and assumed to be understood by readers of the London *Times* in 1924); mortality decline could continue in the better ordered world promised after the Second World War, while fertility was likely to decline only if the modern nations also shared that part of their culture inimical to the fundamental nature of the agrarian economy. He made the point clearer in the subsequent discussion:

> The social-economic ingredients are fairly clear. Probably nothing would help more than rapid urbanization and industrialization. However, popular education, growing political participation, improved health, active birth-control propaganda, rising levels of material welfare, weakened caste and class lines, all would help stimulate parents to new aspirations for themselves and their children—aspirations that are incompatible with large families. Even such changes would not bring quick results.[60]

A little later he returned to 'the more important matter'—

the means by which values centering around the large family may be deflected to those centering around the development of the individual human being.'[61] Emphasis here is given to Notestein and his group because they were to be central in later advice provided in the technical aid field. There were others but the message was essentially similar. Warren Thompson published *Population and Peace in the Pacific* in 1946, emphasizing the new evidence of growth but adding a pessimistic Malthusian note when discussing continued mortality decline in Asia.[62] Similarly, in the same year, Kingsley Davis wrote: 'All told, the melancholy conclusion is reached that an early decline of fertility in India seems unlikely unless rapid changes not now known or envisaged are made in Indian life.'[63] In 1947, C. P. Blacker published a more segmented and even more mechanistic version of demographic transition theory.[64] However, the most interesting aspect of his discussion was the clear influence of an additional year or two's experience of planning for the development of the post-war world. He reported:

> The demographic disequilibrium of the world to-day is surely its biggest long-term problem. For the standards of living prevailing among the high stationary and the early expanding peoples of Asia are far below those of the remaining peoples. Yet we are to-day assuming a collective responsibility to raise these standards. The World Food and Agricultural Organisation (FAO) has been formed and a new morality is being preached. Sir John Boyd Orr has said that 'Any government which will not accept in principle the policy of aiding the starving world should not be considered a Government and should not be allowed to continue.' But have we realized the implications of this revolutionary statement?[65]

Nevertheless, the belief that nothing very dramatic was going to occur with regard to either mortality or fertility was still the dominant view in 1948. In that year Vogt wrote in his *Road to Survival*

One of the greatest obstacles in our path is lack of positive control of populations by sharp reductions of birth rates. . . . If Britain . . . could help bring this problem before the United Nations and develop an action program that would cure the malady there is little doubt but that other nations would follow her lead.[66]

Nevertheless, he was mostly pessimistic.

British withdrawal from India may well result in the reversal of the population trend that this country so badly needs if her people are ever to achieve a reasonably decent standard of living. The spectacle will not be pleasant to watch. How much better it would have been for the people of India if a controlled birth rate could have held her population at a low enough level.[67]

But he did not think that this could be done. 'In areas like Puerto Rico . . . current contraceptive techniques cannot possibly be effective; Hindus, . . . more in need of birth control than any other people, cannot possibly afford contraceptive devices.'[68]

This period culminated in the survey trip made to the Far East in late 1948 by Frank Notestein, Marshall Balfour, Roger Evans and Irene Taeuber, with the support of the Rockefeller Foundation and at the behest of John D. Rockefeller III.[69] The Mission was to report on both public health and demography and the former at least reflected over forty years of Rockefeller Foundation involvement in China.[70] However, the only previous involvement in demography had been institutional grants to the Scripps Foundation and the Office of Population Research from 1944.[71] The Mission visited Japan, Korea, China, Taiwan, Indonesia, and the Philippines. They concluded, even in the text of the published report which came out in 1950, that death rates would not fall easily in most of these countries because of poverty and the density of rural populations.[72]

Nevertheless, they believed that there was evidence of

'population growth likely to endanger sustained advances in human welfare.'[73] This was not likely to change quickly for 'the decline of fertility awaits changes that will both stimulate the desire for fewer children and improve means for fulfilling that desire.'[74] They were not even optimistic that the Eugenics Law in Japan would lead to any marked control of fertility there.[75] They came away with three main impressions. The first was that the most important contribution that could be made by the West and by foundations was research on interrelationships within a changing culture, especially on reasons for wanting children and motives for reducing fertility. 'Study should be emphasized as opposed to direct ameliorative action.'[76] The second was the need to create an indigenous body of scholars and other experts. 'We believe that interest and knowledge will be deepened mainly by the work of Far Easterners studying their own problems by modern means and that sound public interest will come mainly as a by-product of expanded work on these problems by Far Eastern students.'[77] The third conclusion was underscored by an experience that remained with Frank Notestein for the rest of his life.

The difficulties of introducing birth control were embarrassingly evident in Peipei, a county northwest of Chungking. Throughout the trip we had probed rather deeply to find interest in birth control. In Peipei the situation was reversed. The mayor and his associates have developed one of the most progressive communities in China. Banditry has been suppressed, agriculture developed and private and co-operative industry encouraged. Most of the children are in school and there are classes for illiterate adults conducted in cooperation with the Mass Education Movement. Work in public health is also under way. The mayor explained that his program lacked only one part—population control. He asked us what we would recommend for birth control. In our search for evidence of interest in birth control we had almost forgotten that we were

bankrupt insofar as realistic recommendations were concerned. We spoke lamely of folk methods [Notestein
usually meant withdrawal when he used this term] and of
what might be done under different economic circum-
stances. But we knew that there was no method of contraception really suitable to the needs of his community.[78]
[They concluded] the main difficulty is that there is no
single contraceptive method that is likely to prove of any
substantial importance to the peasant population of
Asia's mainland. Any such method must be very cheap,
simple, safe and effective. So far as we know such a
method neither exists nor is on the horizon. Moreover
relatively little attention has been given to the problem
anywhere in the world. It is one that could be attacked
immediately and in the West. We doubt that any other
work offers a better opportunity for contributing to
Asia's and the world's fundamental problems of human
welfare.[79]

These three themes, demographic research within a social
science context, the preparation of Third World experts in
the population field, and biomedical research aimed at easier
birth control, were to be the major elements of future
funding operations in the population field.

Yet that time had not yet quite arrived. Although the
Study Committee under the chairmanship of H. Rowan
Gaither, jun., set up to report on the future of the Ford
Foundation in terms of policy and program, reported as
late as November 1949 that 'The Foundation was established
for the general purpose of advancing human welfare',[80] and
that the greatest problems to be faced were social ones,[81]
there was no mention of population. The main reason was
that the emphasis was still amost entirely on the United
States. Between the end of the 1940s on one hand and
1952 on the other something quite dramatic happened both
to the West's attitudes to population and to the Ford Foundation's stance with regard to the Third World. It is of prime

importance for our understanding of the later period to determine exactly what happened at the beginning of the 1950s.

Much of what occurred lay right outside the population field but it had major implications for technical aid and for changing the world. The colonial regimes which may have been efficient in reducing mortality but which posed problems in terms of the decay of indigenous supports for high fertility (as interpreted by the Princeton OPR group) began to disappear with a suddenness that had not been foreseen during the Second World War. The Philippines achieved independence in 1946, followed by India and Pakistan in 1947. By 1949, Indonesia's sovereignty was recognized, and the 1952 coup in Egypt broke the final British ties there. These were the very countries that demographers in previous decades had chiefly written about. At the same time, the continued erection from 1945 onward of the United Nations system and the mediation it offered between the industrialized countries and the newly independent Third World nations gave fair promise that mortality would be at least as efficiently confined as before and that there might be some possibility of acting against high fertility. Furthermore, it became clear that the world was moving into an era of unprecedented, and largely unforeseen, technical aid. This was partly catalyzed by a series of dramatic political events: the beginning of the Cold War in 1947, the success of the communist revolution in China in 1949, and the outbreak of the Korean War in 1950. The new Third World nations began to be important in a world that was growing politically more competitive and which interpreted that competition in terms of economic assistance and economic development.

Massive technical aid began, not to the Third World, but to Europe under the Marshall Plan of 1948–53. However, this provided the precedent and the stimulus for the Point Four Progam which started in 1950. The Marshall Plan was administered by the United States Economic Cooperation Administration which was headed by Paul Hoffman until he moved to the Presidency of the Ford Foundation in 1951. The Ford Foundation became massively involved in Third World development programs from 1952, partly because of the inclinations of Hoffmann and partly because of the rapidly increasing belief in Third World development. Nevertheless, India had played a role and Nehru had set the process going by asking the Foundation for assistance, and it is no accident that overseas assistance began with South Asia and the Middle East.

However, there was an important specific demographic element in all this. Some of it had to do with actual population numbers. In the late 1940s it was realized just how rapid population growth was in Sri Lanka, Taiwan, the Caribbean, and Puerto Rico.[82] However, the most salutary shock was provided both to Prime Minister Nehru and to persons involved in development planning around the world when the 1951 Indian Census figures were released in early 1951 showing a total population of 361 millions, evidence that sustained population growth had continued for a third straight decade and that the 1941–51 growth rate had approximated the record growth of 1931–41 (at around 14 percent per decade). Later, this experience was to be repeated even more dramatically for China. The United Nations Demographic Yearbook for 1954 showed against China a population of 463 millions, noting that this was a 1948 estimate. However, with the release of figures for the 1953 Census, the 1955 Year Book presented a figure of 583 million, noting that this was for 1953.

However, the major change in outlook during this period probably arose more from pictures of the future than from the measurement of the present. The experience of two decades of producing component population projections, mostly to show the dire results of declining birth rates in the West, was now employed to demonstrate the potential for very great growth in the Third World. What is so ironic about the earlier estimates is just how low they were compared with the reality that was to follow. It was these relatively low estimates that spurred efforts to attempt to avoid catastrophe; we now feel that if population growth had really been so moderate economic development might have been relatively easy. In 1944, Clyde Kiser warned that a geometrical increase in Egypt's population would yield a population in 1970 of 24 millions.[83] He concluded that this probably could not be attained and that the population in 1970 was likely to be 18–21 millions; in fact it was 33 millions. In the same year, Kingsley Davis warned that if India repeated the Western demographic transition in time and magnitude, then its population would reach 750 millions by the year 2024;[84] in fact the population of the subcontinent (India, Pakistan, and Bangladesh) reached that level in 1975. In 1945, Frank Notestein wrote that 'sensible planning for the future should be based on the assumption that the world will have at least 3 billion people by the year 2000';[85] in fact the population will probably be almost twice that and the increase during five and a half decades five times that predicted. In 1949, Irene Taeuber wrote of 'Alice-in-Wonderland' early Second World War German 'estimates that the earth could support eight or nine billion people two or three centuries hence;'[86] no one now assumes that these levels will not be reached and it is believed that they will be attained around 2025.[87]

The major impact on world thinking was to come from projections released by the United Nations. In 1946, the United Nations had established an Economic and Social Council, under which there was a Population Division guided by a Population Commission and a Statistical Office guided by a Statistical Commission. The Population Division was headed first by Frank Notestein, on leave from Princeton University's Office of Population Research, then by Pascal Whelpton, on leave from the Scripps Foundation, and more permanently by John Durand, the first student of the Office of Population Research. The Statistical Office resumed the practice of producing periodic volumes of world population estimates with the *1947 Demographic Year Book*. However, a major advance was the production of the *1949–50 Demographic Year Book* with reconstructed estimates of the 1949 population. The United Nations began to make improved estimates of recent population trends with its *World Economic Report, 1948*[88] and improved these at the very end of the 1940s when the Department of Social Affairs published *World Population Trends, 1920–1947.*[89] The latter showed population growth for the decade 1937–47 to be only 8.5 percent for both the whole world and Asia but to be 18.6 percent for Africa and 21.4 percent for Latin America (this being before the new census figures for India and China). In 1951, the Population Division published its first *Population Bulletin* which provided three estimates for the 1980 population of the world showing that it was highly likely that the world would reach the 3 billion mark before 1980.[90] The Low, Medium, and High Projections for 1980 were 2,976 millions, 3,277 millions, and 3,636 millions respectively. In reality, the 1980 population was 4,415 millions and the increase between 1950 and 1980 was over 2 billions, or almost four times that projected by the Low estimate and not far short of double that anticipated by the High estimate. In fact, the High estimate was not far out for either the group consisting of North America, Western Europe, and Oceania (overstated by 2 percent) or the group consisting of Latin America, Japan, Eastern Europe, and USSR (overstated by 8 percent). The huge error lay in the general belief of the time that mortality could not fall precipitously in Asia or Africa and the real population of this group in 1980 was 42 percent or almost one billion above even the High projection. Since then the Population Division has released seven more sets of population projections.[91] What disconcerted demographers in the 1950s was not so much how high the projections were but how rapidly population growth was outstripping our ability to project it. Each projection revealed that the Third World was growing faster than previously predicted because of the demonstration provided by population censuses that death rates were being

pushed down faster than public health experts had anticipated. The Medium projection for the world's population in
1980 was 3,277 millions in 1950, 3,628 millions in 1954,
4,220 millions in 1958, 4,330 millions in 1963, and 4,457
millions in 1968, after which it plateaued while the world's
population actually attained 4,415 millions in 1968. The
major stimulus to action in the early 1950s was the early
projections themselves; the stimulus in the late 1950s, when
the Ford Foundation entered the field in a major way, was
both the level of the much higher projections and the fact
that they had increased by a billion people over eight years.
But even the first United Nations projection convinced
Notestein that the 3.3 billion world population that had
been repeatedly reproduced as the Office of Population
Research estimate for the end of the century would instead
be reached by 1980 and that something nearer 5 billions was
more likely for 2000.

By the beginning of the 1950s something was already
known about fertility control in non-industrialized societies.
Paul Hatt, encouraged by conversations while at the Office
of Population Research in 1946-7, had taken the Indianapolis
Survey methodology to Puerto Rico in 1947-8 and had
shown that a completed family size of around six children
hid the fact that many women would have preferred smaller
families if that had been possible.[92] In 1951-2, one of the
supervisors in that project, J. Mayone Stycos, was back in
the island interviewing working-class families in depth and
concluding that, although there was some demand for the
restriction of family size, of the birth control methods then
available only sterilization seemed to have much chance of
success.[93] There had been some government provision of
family planning in Puerto Rico through pre-maternal clinics
since the 1930s and the island was, during the 1950s and
1960s, to be almost as influential with Americans interested
in controlling high fertility as had been the case of India
with British thinking.

The new attitudes crystallized in 1952 with a paper by

Notestein to the International Conference of Agricultural Economists,[94] the holding of a kind of crisis conference at Williamsburg organized by John D. Rockefeller 3rd and funded by the Rockefeller Foundation, and the establishment of the Population Council. What happened between the publication of the 1948 Far East trip in 1950 and 1952 remains partly conjectural. Rockefeller was accustomed to taking initiatives and probably regarded the 1950 report as too passive. It was certainly he who moved for the Williamsburg meeting once the Rockefeller Foundation had expressed its reluctance to take the lead in the population area. Nevertheless, by 1952 Notestein regarded the state of knowledge in 1950 as well back in time, and it was he who arrived at the Williamsburg meeting with a clear concept that there should be a separate small foundation (a foundation's foundation) and of what it could do in the area. These ideas were, of course, very largely those emerging from the Far East trip report, but were now expressed, as in his 1952 paper, in a much more action-orientated way. The explanation for this change was probably no more complex than the fact that the beginning of massive Third World technical aid had demonstrated that demographers could begin to commute to developing countries, to live there, and to command substantial funds. A point of seminal importance, which had been noted by Notestein earlier in the year in a report[95] and which profoundly influenced Rockefeller, was Nehru's announcement that India would establish a national family planning program. Birth control had come within the potential sphere of technical aid. Related too was the meeting at that time in Bombay of the family planning associations of Britain, Holland, Hong Kong, India, Singapore, Sweden, West Germany, and the United States, which founded the International Planned Parenthood Federation. The previous year the International Union for the Scientific Study of Population had set up a Committee on Population Problems of Countries in Process of Industrialization. Notestein had never been conscious of any clash between academic analysis and programatic action, at least if it were the former that influenced the latter,[96] and had been only too happy for the Stix and Notestein analysis to guide the Sanger clinics. He tended to regard the fertility control intervention as social experiments with social value but also as the very essence of what should interest social scientists in their observational work.[97]

In his 1952 paper,[98] Notestein showed that, in contrast to the 1950 Report, he was now convinced that the Japanese birth rate was in sustained decline, quoting a recent paper by Taeuber and Balfour,[99] and that Japan would complete the demographic transition, proving that it was not solely a European phenomenon. He argued that not only were colonial powers unlikely to make dependent people anything but defensive and protective about their high fertility mores but that their success in promoting agriculture had strengthened the traditional family and the social context of high fertility. He quoted the *1949–50 Demographic Year Book* as evidence that growth rates could reach 2–3 percent per annum during the rest of the century, contrasting this with previous assumptions of only 1 percent, provided that economic plans were successful. He developed the proposition of what was to become known later as the 'low level equilibrium trap', arguing that the only things that might prevent mortality falling sufficiently to make these growth rates possible were the Malthusian effects of the growth rates themselves. Like Malthus, he saw only one way out of the vicious cycle and that was by reducing fertility, concluding that 'It is in this tense situation that the resolution of long-run problems requires the stimulation of social change.' He also drew on Wilbert Moore to argue that the destruction of the large traditional family was necessary not only for its indirect effect on economic growth via the reduction of fertility but also for its direct effect in producing a society more attuned to the modern economy.[100] The paper argued both for research and for experimental social engineering: raising the age of marriage, spreading the practice of birth control, noting that an 'intensive programme of public education, coupled with competent technical advice, might accomplish a great deal' because of the existence of unwanted births even in agrarian societies, and the giving of 'prestige to families with educated children', together with the spread of the 'ideal of a few healthy children'. Widespread studies were needed, preferably by indigenous scholars.

> It is quite possible that we can learn to speed the reduction of fertility with something of the efficiency with which we already reduce mortality. . . . If there is a moral to this analysis for the economist, it lies in the fact that he should stray from the well-worn and familiar paths if he is to be truly useful. . . . In view of the demographic situation, his hopes for long-run success in ameliorating living conditions must lie in speeding the change of institutions.

The remaining events of 1952 were subsequently to be important but were given very little publicity at the time. The Williamsburg Conference produced no publication and was noted in neither *Population Index* nor *The Milbank Memorial Fund Quarterly*. The incorporation of the Population Council in the state of New York late in the year went so unnoticed that it had to be drawn to the attention of the Ford Foundation the following year. The Council began major activities only from its first Ford Foundation Grant in 1954.

Spurred by events, especially those in India, demographers took readily to the idea of intervention to lower the birth rate and of changing social institutions. Kingsley Davis wrote in 1953:

> India is currently engaged in a massive experiment fraught with the greatest human significance. She is attempting through government action to lower the birth rate quickly in a predominantly rural Asian population of 370 million. If the experiment succeeds, it will point the way to similar action in other overcrowded and impoverished areas of the world—areas which embrace at least half of mankind.

India's lead may thus help to solve one of the worst afflictions of modern times, the aimless and economically deleterious multiplication of human numbers.[101]

Frank Lorimer, in an important study relating society and its culture to fertility, concluded in 1954 that,

> it is by no means impossible that socially directed movements, sometimes with government sponsorship, led by intellectual, social and religious leaders, teachers, physicians and councils, such as the panchayats in India, may play a far larger role in this sphere of human interests [the reduction of fertility] in Asia than has been the case in Europe.[102]

On the international scene the work of this period culminated in the publication by the UN Population Division in 1953 of an influential volume, *The Determinants and Consequences of Population Trends: A Summary of the Findings of Studies on the Relationships between Population Changes and Social and Economic Conditions*[103] and the 1954 World Population Conference, organized under the auspices of the United Nations, with its Population Division collaborating with the IUSSP, and also with FAO, the World Bank, ILO, UNESCO, and WHO. In some ways it was the end of an era, being dominated by population projections and having few Third World field studies and none of fertility control experiments.[104]

By 1955 the Population Division had organized the Bandung Seminar in the conference hall in West Java which had been built a year earlier for the Bandung Conference of developing countries. Here, more than in Rome, the question of demographic training for Third World students became prominent.[105]

The major intellectual effort of the mid-1950s was on the interrelation between population growth and economic development, all studies influencing policy by concluding that rapid population growth retarded economic development and was dangerous for reasons other than the threat to outrun the food supply. It might be noted that this really was a post-Malthusian argument, but it might also be noted that the debate then entered has not yet been resolved.[106] The major writings were those of Richard Nelson in 1956 on 'the low-level equilibrium trap,'[107] Harvey Leibenstein's *Economic Backwardness and Economic Growth*[108] in 1957, and the 1958 book by Ansley Coale and Edgar Hoover, *Population Growth and Development in Low-Income Countries*.[109] Significantly, the last work was funded by the World Bank.

By March 1959, in response to a specific request from the Sixth International Conference on Planned Parenthood in Delhi the previous month, the United Nations Population Commission took up the issue.

> The Commission said that it was necessary to raise frankly the question whether in some of these countries population growth has reached such a point as to make economic development more difficult or slower in its progress, or to make it dependent on special kinds of measures . . . The Commission recommended that the United Nations shift the emphasis of its work from the improvement and the coverage of demographic information to aiding countries in the study of the interrelations of population growth, vital rates and population structure on the one hand with economic and social development on the other.[110]

Meanwhile, Third World fertility surveys, the predecessors of the KAP surveys of the 1960s and the WFS surveys of the 1970s, were beginning to spread. Surveys were undertaken in Jamaica in 1953[111] and again in 1956–7.[112] Beyond the Caribbean, C. Chandrasekaran had been in the field in south India in 1951–2.[113] The latter survey was important for several reasons: its substantial scope, the fact that it was a United Nations Population Division undertaking, and its significance in establishing a Delhi office which served as a conduit for Chandrasekaran participating in the important population subcommittee for India's First Five Year Plan and for reports to that committee being received from Pascal Whelpton, Kingsley Davis, and William Ogburn.

By 1959, too, the demography profession had developed to the point where its structure and achievements could be catalogued. In that year, Philip Hauser and Otis Dudley Duncan published *The Study of Population: An Inventory and Appraisal*, which had been commissioned by the National Science Foundation in 1954 as part of a series of reports being 'the necessary first step in policy development.[114]

Ford Foundation population activities in the 1950s

So far we have concentrated on the demographic profession. Later, when considering broader struggles over policy, we will retrace some of our steps. For the moment, we will focus more specifically on the Ford Foundation and go back no further than the early 1950s.

The central question of interest is not why the Ford Foundation entered the population field in the 1950s but why it did not mount a large-scale program until the very end of the decade. Part of the answer lies in a somewhat surprising caution and part in the existence of the Population Council which at first fulfilled some of the functions of a front but later probably hastened the massive involvement of the Foundation in the population field.

The 1949 Gaither Study Committee saw the Foundation's future as being largely concerned with internal American matters. At home the emphasis was to be on the improvement of the society and the strengthening of its economy. The outside world was seen largely in terms of improving the prospects for peace. Population does not enter the Report even by implication.[115]

Thirty years later, Richard Magat was to state that the 1950 Report covered nearly everything which was later done: 'Among the few exceptions are our work in the arts, family planning, and the prevention of drug abuse.'[116] This judgement is sound enough with reference to fields of interest but does less than justice to the change in balance of work to assist in the development of the Third World. Magat makes two further important points. The first is that the Foundation restated its objectives in 1962 but in such a way that the listed fields were illustrative and not restrictive.[117] He also listed in order the influences which led the Foundation to choose new objectives.[118] That of outside persons or organizations is mentioned last, but this was certainly not the case with regard to population where the external demand by the end of the 1950s was very considerable.

Although the Ford Foundation had existed in Michigan since 1936, the Foundation in its present form emerged only in 1950. By the end of that year Paul Hoffmann had defined South and Southeast Asia and the Middle East as areas for Foundation concern and funds had been appropriated for the Overseas Development Program in these areas. Africa was not added until 1958; and Latin America and the Caribbean in the following year.

Francis Sutton said that 'foundations are constantly scrutinizing the landscape to find directions in which they have a comparative advantage.'[119] There was certainly to be a case of comparative advantage in the population field for it was not until the mid-1960s that governments lost their apprehension of what they regarded as a controversial matter both at home and abroad. Ultimately, the Rockefeller Foundation was to prove even more reluctant than the Ford Foundation to follow up their involvement in the medical and public health fields with any significant funding for fertility control in spite of the efforts of John D. Rockefeller 3rd. Nevertheless, the Rockefeller Foundation provided the funds for the Conference that John D. Rockefeller organized in Williamsburg in 1952. This meeting heard a range of papers which presented essentially the viewpoint which had emerged from the Princeton Office of Population Research during the 1940s and which was finally formulated in Notestein's 1953 paper to the Agricultural Economists.[120] Although the push for activism came more from Rockefeller than Notestein, the design for a Population Council was largely the product of the latter after discussion with Frederick Osborn.

In 1952 the Ford Foundation made its first population grant—one to the Population Reference Bureau to support the *Population Bulletin* for three years. The year was an important one for the Foundation in terms of the beginning of major funding for American universities and this included the establishment of foreign-area studies and centers.

Both the February and June 1953 meetings of the Ford Foundation Trustees were presented at considerable length with reports on rapid population growth in the Third World and on the need for intervention. Indeed, the June meeting believed that $500,000 per year might be spent on population matters in the Third World through existing institutions, provided that none was spent on the biomedical or family planning areas. In fact, the only expenditure in that year was a grant in 1953 of $40,000 to the IUSSP to allow the payment of delegates' fares to the World Population Conference in Rome the following year.

Some of the Foundation Trustees were strongly interested in planned parenthood but were apprehensive, apparently wrongly, of Henry Ford II's views. Richard Magat believes that the basic problem was broader. 'The Joseph R. McCarthy era and the congressional investigations of foundations took their toll of the Ford Foundation and no doubt helped to account for our caution, especially in the late 1950s, in approaching anything with great potential for controversy.[121]

The Population Council had been incorporated on November 17, 1952 but this was not publicly announced until August 1953 and it commenced operations with staff on September 1, 1953, although a few small grants had already been made with the authorization of Frederick Osborn and Frank Notestein. However, discussions with the Ford Foundation, with a view to future funding, began as early as April 15, 1953, with a lunch at the Century Association between Waldemar Neilsen and Frederick Osborn. A second lunch, on June 26, 1953, included also Bernard Berelson, then with the Ford Foundation, when Osborn said that emphasis was being given to setting up a headquarters, establishing a fellowship program, and beginning research on psychological and demographic matters. The first field research would be in

Japan and Puerto Rico and there would be a study of twins in the United States. Berelson was subsequently to be the major contact with the Population Council as head of the foundation's experimental Behavioral Science Program which was given responsibility for population.

On February 10, 1954, Osborn lodged with the Ford Foundation a request for a grant of $600,000 to be spent over 3 to 5 years for training and research on economic, social and psychological aspects of population growth with special regard to developing countries. He explained that the Population Council also intended to finance biomedical research but would not use Ford Foundation funds for that purpose. The Population Council had already received $1,300,000 from various monies to which John D. Rockefeller 3rd had access. Until that date the Council had been operating at the level of about $250,000 per annum, and grants had been divided into 39 percent for research, 29 percent for fellowships, 21 percent for international conferences, in addition to other miscellaneous allocations. The large amount for conferences was explained by preparations for the coming meeting in Rome. The population field still carried its history with it. Osborn, in one of the last gasps of the Eugenics tradition, informed the Ford Foundation that the Population Council would also be interested in the qualitative aspects of population matters. Most of the first research grants went to the Milbank Memorial Fund and the Scripps Foundation for studies of differential fertility and population projections although the University of Puerto Rico did receive money for the field interviews being undertaken by Stycos on fertility and fertility attitudes.

The funding request emphasized the importance the Population Council placed on fellowships which would allow foreign students to study in America or abroad, pointing out that unless the Ford Foundation came to the rescue the Council would be able to afford only six fellowships per year. The Population Council followed Frank Notestein's prescription in its choice of geographical emphasis and referred to the great need for 'centers of training and research overseas.' This emphasis was explained in terms of the different cultural conditions found in other parts of the world.

The Ford Foundation acceded to the request making $600,000 available over the next five years and continued to make grants to the Population Council, amounting by 1960 to $2,500,000 with a further $3,800,000 pledged. From 1955 Berelson negotiated with the Population Council and with John Durand, Head of the United Nations Population Division, for Foundation money to be employed either indirectly through the Population Council or later directly for the United Nations Demographic Centres in Bombay, India, and Santiago, Chile. By January 1957 he was arguing in a memo to the Trustees the need

> to provide support . . . for one or more training centers in the United States or possibly in Western Europe to give specialized advanced training to a limited number of students from underdeveloped areas. The expectation would be that this nucleus of well-trained native scientists would in time provide leadership for indigenous research, training and action programs in the home areas.

He also argued for the augmentation of fellowship programs and steered through the Foundation a three-year grant to the Population Council which was approved in March 1957. Later in 1957 Berelson left Ford and the Behavioral Science Program was dissolved. The reasons were complex and could not be summed up by the legend within the Foundation that this was a punishment for being too adventuresome by in-directly financing, through the National Science Foundation, the work of Alfred Kinsey on human sexuality, thereby up-setting some of the Foundation's trustees. Nevertheless, the legend was to be remembered by Foundation staff when they again returned to human reproduction.

Nevertheless, during the 1950s, the Ford Foundation spent over $300,000 per annum on the Population Council, and indeed provided about half of the Council's budget until the mid-1960s. Much of this expenditure provided an institutional and human infrastructure that the Ford Foundation was to draw upon once it entered the field directly.

One of the periodic spurts that has marked the population field occurred in 1959. On March 25, 1959 Thomas Carroll wrote to Mrs Fisher that 'the Ford Foundation expects to keep in close touch with development in the [population] field.' Five days earlier, the Ford Foundation had approved a five-year grant to the Population Council, this time to expand both demographic and medical work. When, in May 1959, it was announced that Frank Notestein would take over the Presidency of the Population Council from July 1, in order to expand the Council's activities, Carroll wrote to Rockefeller assuring him of the Ford Foundation's enthusiastic support.

Nevertheless, the kind of support the Foundation had been channeling left the field underfinanced and in some ways developing fastest at the geographical periphery where Notestein had believed that the critical change must take place. Fellowships were outrunning training facilities. The Foundation did at last move, but to understand that move we must look first at three different areas of change: India, the United Nations Demographic Centres, and attitudes in the United States.

The unique role of India

It is hard to exaggerate the role of India in promoting interest in population questions. It was for long the only large, poor, densely settled country for which there were adequate statistics. Until well into this century it gave most observers the impression that it was the archetypical example of Malthusian equilibrium. An extraordinary proportion of the families which produced Britain's intellectual elite had experience of India or connections with it. Thomas Malthus taught at the East India Company's College, while both John Stuart Mill and Maynard Keynes worked for the India Office.

Perhaps the most valuable demographic data that exist are the one-hundred-year series provided by the Indian Census. Not only were there copious tables for both the whole country and its constituent parts, but the Provinces and later the States had their separate series of reports. The Census takers were literate, well-educated men and many of the ideas taken up by anthropologists and demographers originated in their analytical prefatory volumes. The 1911 Census attempted to relate the cultivable area in different parts of India to the rate of population growth in order to explore Malthusian pressures. The 1921 Superintendent of the Census, J. T. Marten deciding that the influenza epidemic was an aberration and unlikely to be repeated, came to the following conclusion:

A systematized attack is being made on mortality at every point both officially and privately by the improvement of sanitation, the extension of medical relief and the organized efforts towards infant and maternal welfare. Any substantial success in such methods would mean the widening of the difference between the birth rate and the death rate and a corresponding rise in the rate of increase of the population. . . . She has abandoned—or more or less abandoned—the old-fashioned methods of limiting population to an optimum, viz. periodic abstention from intercourse, abortion and infanticide and she has not yet adopted the methods of advanced countries, viz. postponement of marriage and voluntary birth control. She is at a point where her population is controlled by disease and disease only.[122]

Marten had been considerably influenced by Carr-Saunders whose book, *The Population Problem*, was published the year after the Census.[123] J. H. Hutton, the Superintendent of the 1931 Census and later the author of a seminal book on caste, wrote in his 1931 Census Report:

It appears to be the general opinion of Indian economists who discuss the population problem of this country that the only practical method of limiting the population is by the introduction of artificial methods of birth control, though it is not easy to exaggerate the difficulties of introducing such methods in a country where the vast majority of the population regard the propagation of male offspring as a religious duty and the reproach of barrenness as a terrible punishment for crimes committed in a former incarnation. . . . Nevertheless, a definite movement towards artificial birth control appears to be taking place and is perhaps less hampered by misplaced prudery than in some countries which claim to be more civilized; thus not only is artificial control publicly advocated by a number of medical writers but Madras can boast a Neo-Malthusian League with two Maharajas, three High Court judges and four or five men very prominent in public life as its sponsors. . . . A move . . . has already been made by the Governor of Mysore State, which in 1930 sanctioned the establishment of birth control clinics in the four principal hospitals of the State.[124]

An appendix to the 1931 Census fitted Pearl's logistic curve to population growth in Bengal,[125] far underestimating the future course of growth there.

At least from the establishment of the three Presidency Colleges in 1851 there had been a two-way flow of ideas between Britain and India, and there was much interest in India in the Neo-Malthusian movement. This was pointedly expressed in India by the publication in 1916 by P. K. Wattal, *The Population Problem in India.*[126] By 1916, a Eugenics Association had been formed at the Madras Presidency College. Two committee members of the Association, the Maharaja of Mysore and Lady Rama Rao, received some of the first ideas that were later to lead respectively to the establishment of the world's first government birth control clinics and the Presidency of the International Planned Parenthood Association.[127] Because of its lack of statistics, China played no comparable role in demographic thinking. In works like Warren Thompson's 1930 book, *Population Problems*[128] and Carr-Saunders's 1936 book, *World Population,*[129] the non-industrialized world was represented by Russia, Japan and India. By 1940, India had at least twenty-one centers providing birth control services and another forty providing information.[130]

In India, as in Japan and China, there were no deeply entrenched moral or religious attitudes against fertility control and discussions were usually very matter-of-fact. There was some Gandhian opposition but it usually took the form of merely registering dissenting votes. From 1935 the All-India Women's Conference annual meetings had passed motions favoring a birth control program, and in 1936 they invited Margaret Sanger to their meeting 'to assist them to "put teeth in it" '.[131] In 1945, the Final Report of the Bengal Famine Inquiry Commission stated that India's growth would add 100 millions to the population in the next quarter of a century unless it were curbed and advocated the imparting of knowledge of birth control through maternal and child welfare centers.[132] The following year the

Government inquiry into public health, the Bhore Committee, brought down four large volumes which included a recommendation for the Government to make available free contraception, the only split in the committee being on whether services should be provided on economic grounds alone.[133] The Committee quoted quite extensively a 1944 paper written by Kingsley Davis.[134] In 1947 a subcommittee of the Congress Party's National Planning Committee, which first met in 1939 but did so more regularly from 1945, published its report in the form of a book, *Population*.[135] The report drew heavily on the census, demographic analyses and population projections. It stated that 'The importance of deliberately controlled numbers cannot be exaggerated in a planned economy.'[136] It recommended government birth control clinics with free contraceptive supplies, the local manufacture of contraceptives, the inclusion of family planning in all medical courses, the in-service training of all doctors and nurses in contraception, and government propaganda for 2 to 4 years' spacing between children and a maximum of four children.[137] In April, 1951, Prime Minister Nehru was advised by the Census Commissioner, R. A. Gopalaswami (who had been the Secretary of the Bengal Famine Inquiry) that the provisional 1951 Census Population was 362 millions. He issued a press statement saying that something would have to be done about population, and, as part of the preparation for the First Five Year Plan to begin in 1952, had a committee appointed by the Panel on Health Programmes in order to consider and report on population growth and family planning.[138] The Committee included both C. Chandrasekaran, who was then heading the United Nations office in Delhi while conducting the Mysore Study, and Gopalaswami. Among other evidence, it considered reports by Kingsley Davis, Pascal Whelpton, and William Ogburn.[139] Within a few months it unanimously recommended a population policy, and, with one dissentient, Dr Sushila Nayar, the Minister of Health, a national family planning program. When releasing the report Nehru announced that the 1952

Plan would include a government family planning program. These events were a bombshell in the previously rather detached population field. Frank Notestein wrote,

> The speed with which the Indian government had been moving toward a policy supporting family planning is quite remarkable. Until recent years it seemed a safe generalization that official recognition of a need for family limitation comes, if at all, only after birth control is the well-established practice of a major proportion of the population.[140]

Gopalaswami, who has remained much more deeply affected by the experience of enquiring into the Bengal famine than discovering the size of the 1951 Census count, wrote an analysis of the implications of India's population growth in his *1951 Census Report* estimating that India was heading for a 1981 population of 520 million, a number which would mean even less adequate feeding than was the case three decades earlier. He presented this analysis, with considerable impact, to the 1954 World Population Conference.[141] As early as 1951 he had informed Nehru that vasectomy was the only answer.

The Indian Government appointed a physician, Colonel B. L. Raina, as head of the program. He had been associated with a family planning clinic in Bombay in the late 1930s and had published a book on birth control. Once he had assumed office, he began to draw on experience accumulated by the army since General Kalipha had introduced family planning for servicemen and their families the previous year, employing Raina's book as a guide. It was in this atmosphere that the 1952 Bombay family planning conference inaugurated the IPPF.

It was inevitable that the Ford Foundation would be drawn into the Indian family planning program. Nehru had encouraged the Foundation to work overseas in 1950 and its operations in India under Douglas Ensminger dwarfed Ford activities anywhere else outside the United States. From

1957, Raina attempted to obtain commitment in the population field both from Ensminger and from Moye Freymann who was working for the Foundation in the public health field. During these two years Raina's requests were treated gingerly in New York so that they were not actually refused. The position became ever more awkward as the Foundation gave greater emphasis in the late 1950s to India's food crises,[142] leading to the emergency funding actions which by 1960 had produced the 'Intensive Agricultural Districts Program.'

The pressure to do something in the population field had mounted since 1955. In that year Leona Baumgartner, then with the New York City Department of Health, and Notestein went on a mission to India, submitting to the Minister of Health in December 1955 their report, 'Suggestions for a Practical Program of Family Planning and Child Care.' By 1958 the Population Council was funding Edwin Driver's field-work for his study of differential fertility in Central India.[143]

As early as May 16, 1957 Ensminger was reported to F. F. Hill that Colonel Raina had talked jointly to him and to Marshall Balfour, representing the Rockefeller Foundation, about developing educational materials for the Indian family planning program. 'I said that we were not at all sure that our respective Foundations would want to directly support programs related to family planning. We did however tell him that we would take the matter up informally.' On May 22, 1959 Ensminger wrote to Raina saying that the Ford Foundation would develop a communications project, partly because Ensminger had interpreted a letter from F. F. Hill written on April 15 as encouraging. By June 10, 1959 Ensminger was writing to New York that he he and Freymann, after consultation with Raina, had worked out a detailed project and that he 'hoped you people will have reached a decision to support the project by the time I reach New York.' By October 1, 1959 the Foundation had agreed and issued a draft agreement emphasizing, 'The goal is to assist in development of research on the problem of educating people to accept family planning practice.'

There had been more general pressure during the year. On February 14, 1959 Nehru opened the Sixth International Conference on Planned Parenthood in Delhi and spoke of India's tremendous population problem, the lack of success of the family planning program, and the need for a major effort. Nehru praised the global efforts of Margaret Sanger. During the next week the *New York Times* gave the meeting considerable publicity, pointing out that 587 of the 750 delegates were Indian and that the Indian experts had called for massive aid in the area. On February 21 the delegates unanimously requested the Secretary-General of the United Nations to bring the world organization into the field of family planning assistance.

By the end of 1959 activities in the Ford Foundation in India had speeded up. On December 2, 1959 Freymann wrote to the Harvard School of Public Health asking whether they could develop courses of a special type needed to train Indians for the country's family planning programs. On March 15, 1960 Ensminger wrote to Wayne Fredericks, noting that Freymann was selecting trainees and had also contacted public health programs at the University of California and the University of North Carolina. He stated: 'It is our feeling that a more flexible program, adapted to the special needs of these trainees, would be more desirable.' There was an anxiety that teachers should have had the required experience in family planning programs, possibly either in Puerto Rico or among American Indians in Arizona or New Mexico. By February 1960 Notestein was reporting that the Indian Government was so certain of plentiful Ford Foundation assistance that it had lost interest in the Population Council.

The United Nations Demographic Centres

From 1954 the move toward training Third World demographers and others on the demography of the Third World began to accelerate. The Population Council awarded its first fellowships, at first in demography. Most of the early awards went to Americans or Indians. During the first half dozen years the majority were taken up at a wide range of American universities which gave only one or two courses which could be described as being in the population field, and most of these were not given by persons with extensive Third World experience. Nearly half the students undertook the one-year course at the Office of Population Research, Princeton, which was taught by Frank Notestein until 1959 and thereafter by Ansley Coale. The heart of this course was demographic transition, increasingly augmented by examples from Third World research and by a growing body of demographic techniques. OPR devised a Certificate for this course. It suited the needs of some students but frustrated many others and their employers by not leading to a graduate degree. A few Third World students did go on to do their doctorate at Princeton but entrance to the OPR course was not taken as evidence of suitability for admission to the economics or sociology graduate degree courses and those programs contained little extra on population.

The paper presented by the United Nations Population branch (it was earlier a Population Division and would be so again) to the 1954 Rome Conference on 'International Measures for Training in Demography' showed by its eclectic nature just how limited were programs in the field. The United Nations provided grants which often allowed the recipients to do no more than spend eight weeks with

the Population Branch in New York City. The paper com-
plained of a vicious circle whereby few people had extensive
training in demography and there were few requests for
technical assistance in the field because Governments did not
normally anticipate such expertise. It was pointed out that,
although the United Nations Technical Assistance Administration received requests in 1953 for 500 experts, only India
and Indonesia sought population experts.

The situation began to change in 1955. On May 27 the
Economic and Social Council requested the Secretary-
General

> To explore the possibility of establishing standing coopera-
> tive relations with qualified scientific institutions in each
> of the major under-developed regions of the world, which
> could serve as centres for studies on population problems
> of importance in the region and for the training of per-
> sonnel in this field of study on a regional basis; and to
> explore the possibilities of cooperation in the programme
> of regional centres of demographic study and training on
> the part of scientific institutions in other regions which
> have highly developed facilities for work in this field, and
> on the part of non-governmental organizations and private
> foundations.

The significant changes since 1954 seem to have been the
decision by the Indian Government that it needed such a
facility, whether national or international, and the intimation
by the new Population Council that it might be prepared
to assist.

In the second half of 1955 the Indian Government invited
Leona Baumgartner and Frank Notestein to constitute a
mission to India to report on population matters. Baumgartner concentrated mostly on family planning and Notestein
on demographic training. In December, 1955 they submitted
to the Minister of Health, Rajkumari Amrit Kaur, their
report, 'Suggestion for a Practical Program of Family Planning
and Child Care.' The report stated, 'Eventually, India needs

several centers that are able to undertake both advanced training and advanced research, but the immediate need is for one such center.'[144] The report contained a fairly clear description of what the Demographic Training and Research Centre at Bombay was to become but there was no mention of possible United Nations' participation. The part of the report which demonstrated the greatest weakness in the field was the appendix describing suitable types of contraception for such a national program, an appendix which did little more than to demonstrate that the contraceptive armory for a Third World program was hardly better than it had been at the time when Notestein and others visited China in 1948.

However, between the time that the mission was in the field and the delivery of its report the United Nations Seminar on Population and the Far East took place in November–December 1955 at Bandung. The Population Branch presented a paper, 'Proposed Regional Centre for Demographic Research and Training', which

> envisaged that the Centre will be set up, with the co-operation of the United Nations, at the seat of a university or other institution conducting research. The sponsors of the Centre would include the United Nations, the host institution, and the government of the host country in which the centre would be located. If desired by these latter parties, interested specialized agencies on non-governmental organization such as the International Union for the Scientific Study of Population might join in the sponsorship.[145]

The paper envisaged a one-year course extendable to a second year for the most capable students and admitting fifteen to twenty trainees from the various countries of the region each year. It urged that organization should begin in only a few weeks' time in early 1956 and that courses should start in July, 1956. The Seminar recommended the establishment of 'a regional centre for demographic research and training in Asia and the Far East along the lines of the plan prepared by the United Nations Secretariat.'[146]

Rather surprisingly, this rapid timetable was kept to. One reason was the provisional decision already made by the Government of India in collaboration with the Sir Dorabji Tata Trust to found such a center.[147] Another reason was the quick injection of Population Council funds as part of the international component and the recruiting of international experts largely at first from the Population Council–OPR network.

By 1957, moves were underway to establish the Latin American center (Centro Latinoamericano de Demografia, or CELADE) in Santiago, Chile. It was not until 1963 that the Cairo Demographic Centre was established, and 1973 before the sub-Saharan centers were operating.

Because the Ford Foundation supplied half the Population Council funds in the 1950s and 1960s it regarded itself as playing a role in the case of the Asian center and a much more specific role with regard to CELADE where the Population Council negotiators checked back at every stage to make sure that earmarked Ford Foundation funding would be available. Of the international money, the United Nations provided about half and the Population Council the other half.[148] The Indian Government made substantial contributions to the Bombay center but the only Latin American contribution to CELADE was the provision by the Chilean Government of accommodation.

By the end of the 1950s it was clear that these centers were producing at least thirty graduates per year, many of whom desired further training in the population field. The early United Nations hopes of such close relationships with a university so as to produce graduate programs leading to a doctorate had not been realized.

Change in public opinion

The Ford Foundation's apprehension about playing a major role in the population field waned as public opinion changed. Much coverage was given to the results of the 1951 Indian Census and Nehru was widely quoted as saying 'We produce more and more food, but we also produce more and more children. I wish we produced fewer children.'[149] As early as September 1948, *The New York Times* had given considerable publicity to the warning by the FAO in September that food production could not keep up with the threatened population growth.[150] *The New York Times* appears to have spoken with more emphasis on population matters from about the time of the 1954 Rome Conference.[151]

Much of the change was, however, occurring in the United States. On May 7, 1954 *The New York Times* reported that Dr John Rock had called for more money to be made available for research 'so that something close to a birth control pill can be invented.' By 1957 there was considerable coverage to a Planned Parenthood Federation announcement that a synthetic steroid tablet had proved successful as a contraceptive in trials in Puerto Rico. However, by far the greatest news coverage in 1958 was given to the finally successful battle to allow New York City hospitals to provide family planning information and services.

Underlying much of the community's viewpoint were changes in individual behavioral patterns. By the end of the 1950s, 80 percent of couples were themselves practicing family planning.[152] In 1959 the World Council of Churches strongly endorsed all methods of birth control as part of the answer to the world-wide population explosion. Nevertheless, Roman Catholic bishops in the United States issued a statement that they would oppose any use of AID funds to promote family planning. It is probably significant that at this time only a minority of American Catholic couples used illicit methods of family planning, in marked contrast to the situation among non-Catholics at that time and among Catholics a decade later.[153]

However, the most important impact on the Ford Foundation during 1959 was almost certainly the release in July, 1959 of the report of the Committee set up to advise on the US Assistance program and headed by General William H. Draper, former American Ambassador to NATO. The Staff Director of the Committee was Joseph Slater, who later joined the Ford Foundation. The Report recommended that the United States Government should make birth control information available to nations that requested it and should help in the formulation of practical programs to meet the serious challenge posed by rapid population increase. Although President Eisenhower reacted with horror, stating that these were matters of great privacy and in the realm of religion (four years later he said that he had been wrong), the issue of major American governmental and institutional involvement in the area never subsequently disappeared and was aired during the 1960 presidential campaign to an extent that would have been inconceivable in the campaign only four years earlier. Adlai Stevenson, Hubert Humphrey and Nelson Rockefeller all advocated the governmental provision of family planning assistance when requested and John Kennedy said his policy would be what was best for the United States.

Twenty-two years spanned the time from the announcement in 1937 by the American Medical Association that family planning had a definite place in medical practice until November 1959 when the American Public Health Association stated that family planning should be an integral part of public health services.

The Ford Foundation enters the population field

In November 1959 The Ford Foundation continued its work in the population area, begun under the Behavioral Sciences program, by assigning Oscar Harkavy, who had been with the Foundation since 1953, responsibility for population activities. It was the end of the pioneering era on limited funds, but it was, nevertheless, still rather a strange twilight period.

Only two nations, India and Pakistan, had actually announced national family planning programs. The international debate sounded as if it were mostly a matter of decision, but it was by no means clear that there were contraceptive techniques that could make such programs effective. There had been limited experience with sterilization in Puerto Rico, India, and Pakistan. There were rumors about oral contraception but the pill was not to be released even in the West until 1960. The two pre-war intra-uterine devices, the Gräfenberg Ring and the Ota Ring, were held to be dangerous and it was still three years before a conference on the Lippes Loop would herald a new era.

For five years the Population Council had been awarding fellowships, most of which were taken up in the United States. The United Nations Demographic Training and Research Centres had begun to graduate trainees two years earlier and it was now clear that many would prefer and professionally would need more advanced training. The Indian Family Planning program was urging Ford Foundation assistance with projects for which many of the participants would need extensive training. The Population Council was assisting projects in Pakistan where the participating American agencies had already pointed out the need for advanced training in the population field. In the United States, however, no graduate program provided a major specialization in population with a range of supporting courses. Outside the United States a few degrees were given by the London School of Economics where the doctorate was largely achieved by dissertation. In Australia the Australian National University had established a Department of Demography for graduate students in 1952 but it had not yet made Third World population change a major focus. In France there were demographic studies for the *deuxième* and *troisième cycles* (approximating Masters and Doctoral levels) but the approach was largely statistical. In spite of debate in the United States about possible governmental involvement, that intervention was by no means certain, and, on a large scale, was still eight years away.

The fundamental problem was that the population field was undercapitalized. There were no substantial funds for biomedical research and little for assisting Third World population programs. A single center in the American university system for excellence in population had been discussed for six or seven years but seemed no nearer to coming into existence. No advance had been made in either India or Latin America for the cooperative development of doctoral programs between the UN Demographic Centres and local universities.

First steps

The Ford Foundation's entrance to direct activities in the population field was so low-key that there are virtually no records of decisions taken or of the envisaged program. This was in keeping with the Foundation's style of work under F. F. Hill, Vice President in charge of overseas development, in the late 1950s. Oscar Harkavy was asked to take over the population post in 1959 after Bernard Berelson's Behavioral Sciences Program was phased out. It appears clear that the direction and scale of subsequent work was very much of his own devising. The only guidelines appears to have been the spoken suggestion that the field was still somewhat controversial both with regard to the views of individual Trustees and public and governmental attitudes. At the same time the Foundation Office in India began supporting family planning because of the initiative taken by the Indian office as a result of requests from and prodding by the Indian Family Planning Programme.

What appears to be clear is that the dramatic expansion of the Foundation's activities in the population field in the early 1960s was largely the initiative of the Foundation's New York office, together with such field personnel as Douglas Ensminger and Moye Freymann in India and Haldore Hanson in Pakistan. Hill undoubtedly supported this expansion. The Foundation gave both moral and financial support to this extension of their activities.

The Ford Foundation established an official Population Program in 1963 and on February 1, 1964 Harkavy was joined by Lyle Saunders, while the third appointment was not made until August, 1965. In all, there were nineteen appointments to the Population Program (although there were never more than eight or nine at any one time), the last being in February 1977, with the program ceasing as a separate office in September 1983. Two years earlier Harkavy began work on child care and survival. The population staff had largely disappeared by 1981.

The unique contribution made to demographic work was the establishment of the first full teaching programs in American universities, which occurred from 1961 to 1963 when there was only one population officer, and the beginning of population programs in the schools of public health in 1964–5, where there were only two officers. This was in keeping with the Foundation's philosophy that its role was to provide leadership by innovational funding rather than by programatic activities.

Part of the explanation is that Harkavy did not come from the population field, his contribution being that of an outstanding administrator. This forced him to take a low-keyed approach which proved to be very effective. He admits to having been apprehensive of telling Notestein of the limited demographic qualifications he brought to the field, so he sought out the next generation of demographers, particular at first Ronald Freedman and Ansley Coale.

Partly because both he and the Foundation were starting at the beginning, Harkavy organized three seminars in 1959 for guidance and to allow those in the field to debate both needs and directions. Inevitably the first seminar was on demography; behavioral science and biomedical aspects followed. Seven years later it was stated that the Foundation's entry into the population field was based on two propositions:

(1) that the observed growth of world population creates serious problems of human welfare, and (2) that control of conception is technically possible and morally proper . . . the idea that people should be able to limit the size of their families without resort to the more austere Malthusian checks has become orthodox modern morality.[154]

Later still, these early population activities were to be described as the best example of the Ford Foundation taking the lead in a field.[155]

Francis Sutton, describing the work of all the large American foundations, has said that they 'brought with them the habits of working with universities, researchers, and professionals of various kinds, with a strong emphasis on selectivity and quality.'[156] The Foundation had worked earliest with universities in the scientific and technical fields, but from 1952 it began to support foreign-area studies and centers,[157] and from 1967 it was to spend over $40 million attempting to improve graduate education in ten leading universities, all of which had major population programs.[158] By April, 1960 it was suspected by those close to the Foundation that Harkavy's first major thrust was going to be to establish demography programs in universities and that he believed both that the need was for training on a very considerable scale and that the Foundation would provide funds on a scale that meant that there was no longer any need to talk about a single center of excellence. The result was that on April 26, 1960 Vincent Whitney, the Chairman of the University of Pennsylvania's Sociology Department and close to New York thinking because of part-time work with the Population Council, lodged an application for $1,200,000 funding over five years to build a major demographic capability at Pennsylvania. In many ways this was most appropriate as the University of Pennsylvania had the oldest and best developed teaching program in population studies in the world. It was deeply entrenched in sociology and in the previous quarter of a century had concentrated on migration, urbanization, and labor force. In one year it produced as Ph.D graduates Sidney Goldstein, Charles Westoff, and Richard Easterlin. It had on its faculty Edward Hutchison and Dorothy Thomas. Yet the University of Pennsylvania application clearly caused considerable worry and was the catalyst of a great deal of thought; it did not gain funding for almost a year. The reasons were clear. The University of

Pennsylvania's Sociology Department had not awarded a high place to either fertility or Third World development. Its application envisaged the growth of demographic studies very much in the formal tradition of the statistical analysis of American official data.

The University of Michigan's Sociology Department had no more overseas experience but Ronald Freedman was beginning to specialize in fertility studies. In 1949 Clyde Kiser and Pascal Whelpton had drawn him into the analysis of the Indianapolis Survey, and he had recruited a band of graduate students including John Kantner, Jeanne Clare Ridley, and Charles Westoff. Freedman had joined Whelpton to direct the 1955 General American Fertility Survey, the first national household fertility survey in the world, which Whelpton hoped would produce sufficiently reliable data on family building plans to allow the construction of better population projections. (Demographers were scarred by their failure to predict the baby boom.) Freedman, whose interest in world fertility change had been spurred by a visit to India, sponsored by the Population Council, and by receiving a student on a Population Council Fellowship, decided in late 1960 to visit the Population Council in New York to see if they could provide $20,000 to expand his program. Dudley Kirk and Parker Mauldin took him instead to the Ford Foundation to talk to Harkavy. Freedman was astonished at how cordially he was received and Harkavy encouraged him to think on a larger scale, emphasizing that the success of an application depended both on its containing plans for a comprehensive program and on the focus being on the Third World.

In early 1961 Freedman submitted a revised budget of $100,000 per annum for three years. At the end of March the Foundation awarded the University of Michigan $500,000 to cover a seven-year period and the University of Pennsylvania $200,000 for five years. Thus, a major Foundation program got under way. The Office of Population Research at Princeton did not come into the Foundation program at this stage, both because it was adequately funded largely by the Rockefeller Foundation and because it did not wish to change its focus from research to teaching. Two further years elapsed before an award was made to the University of Chicago, while it was not until the 1970s that the demography programs at Brown University and Gerogetown University were funded. Some programs, such as those at the University of Wisconsin and Duke University, continued to concentrate on the United States and never applied. Cornell University had Population Council and other funding and successfully sought some Foundation funds in 1962, 1967 and 1973 but never aimed at becoming particularly large.

An immediate concern was the pool of talent available to allow these demographic programs and later those in the schools of public health to expand rapidly. The enlargement of this pool became an early objective of the programs and a justification for encouraging more graduate students. Yet the real need was for persons with considerable experience in the Third World. In the event no severe bottleneck occurred. The following examples demonstrate the origins of some of the more prominent individuals in the pool of human resources.

There were those like Kirk and Coale who had worked in the Office of Population Research during the early 1940s. In addition, many of the OPR and Scripps Foundation people had been taken to Japan by the Occupation Administration in the late 1940s. There were those like Freedman, Kantner, Ridley, Westoff, Albert Hermalin, and David Goldberg, who had had experience with either the Indianapolis Survey or the 1955 GAF Survey. Some had been overseas with American Government projects, often involved with the upgrading of statistical services with a population element as in the case of Philip Hauser's period in Burma in 1951–2 and Nathan Keyfitz's visits to Indonesia from 1953 onwards. Jason Finkle spent 1959–60 in Vietnam on a research program on rural local government. The Ford Foreign Area Program had brought Frederic Shorter into South Asian and then Turkish interests in the 1950s, while

Moye Freymann had worked on public health with the Ford Foundation in India. Donald Bogue and Dorothy Thomas had been sent with Population Council contracts to the UN Demographic Training and Research Centre in Bombay. The Population Council's project in Pakistan led to Paul Harper visiting from 1958 and Leslie Corsa working there in 1962-3, and that in Thailand gave Allan Rosenfield his experience. The Rockefeller Foundation's Khanna Project provided experience in the Punjab from the early 1950s for John Wyon, John Gordon, and others at Harvard University, as well as Carl Taylor and, in the analysis with Ford Foundation support, for Robert Potter from 1963. Population Council fellowships laid the foundation in the Third World with Tangoantiang (later N. Iskandar) coming to the United States from Indonesia and Saad Gadalla from Egypt, although the latter had previous experience with the Ford Foundation's Nubian Project in the study of migration. In contrast, Mercedes Concepcion received her first demographic training at the University of Sydney, Australia, and went to the University of Chicago later after attending the 1955 Bandung Seminar.

Harkavy regarded the United States as the chief resource base but also he was largely confined there because of the Ford Foundation's structure whereby the Third World came under regional representatives. Even before Harkavy held the three original population seminars he had set off for India to examine the population situation there. Clearly he was influenced most by four experiences. The first was a period with Colonel Raina, Moye Freymann, and the Indian Family Planning Programme in which the Ford Foundation had recently given the go-ahead for a communications project. The second was a visit to the Khanna Study in the Punjab which had then been proceeding for almost seven years. The third was a short period with the UN Demographic Training and Research Centre in Bombay at a time when Donald Bogue was the foreign consultant, two years after the first students had graduated with certificates and one year after the first diplomas had been awarded. The final visit was to Gandhigram in south India where a community experiment in public health had been developed with Foundation assistance and where there were now thoughts of extending the work to family planning. The Gandhigram experiment, and its early claims of quite dramatic success in achieving considerable levels of family planning acceptance and significantly lowering the birth rate, was going to have a considerable impact on thinking in the population field.

Back in New York, early 1961 saw the final negotiations with the Universities of Pennsylvania and Michigan which would mold the form which later university population programs took.

The first population programs

Ford Foundation money in the population field, as in other fields, went to a small number of well-known universities. There was always a concept of excellence and of finding the right person and the right institution for the job. Curiously, this was to influence Third World administrations in that a man who returned with views he had learnt at Harvard or Chicago was more likely to be taken seriously than if he had been trained at a more obscure center.

All the institutions that received Foundation money in the early 1960s now attest that they were able to do so much with it because it was so flexible and with so few strings. They make the comparison not only with later governmental spending but also with Foundation funding in the 1970s and 1980s as the Foundation's population program developed. The Foundation's major aim was stated when funding the population program at the University of Michigan.

> The institutional base of population study in the United States is too small to meet the growing need for qualified personnel and technical assistance on population projects, especially in the less developed areas. . . . The need for trained demographers has been greatly intensified by the growing interest in population problems in less developed areas and especially by the development of national policies favoring population control.

Yet, the Ford Foundation neither provided money for the hiring of teaching staff nor the provision of new courses, nor did it normally fund the research projects of faculty who had been attracted into the population field. Direct intervention into university teaching programs would have been fraught with danger and might well have been very time-consuming. Instead, the chief thrust was to finance population centers usually at least partially independent from departments. This strategy was partly learnt from the earlier Foundation establishment of Foreign Area Study Programs. The approach worked remarkably well, even though it depended on reciprocal moves within the universities which are not stated formally in any of the funding documents. Two points should be made. Foundations always prefer to work in this way so that some pump-priming attracts other financing and leads to a chain of activities. In addition, universities, and especially their graduate schools, were still growing rapidly in 1960. The development of graduate programs, especially doctoral programs, had to a very considerable extent been a postwar process, and in the social sciences was still not complete in the early 1960s. This was particularly so with regard to specializations and it seemed appropriate that additional courses should be added to provide for those who wished to work in the population field.

Teaching continued in most cases to be done by the departments. The Centers were the part-time home of faculty members from one or more departments who were interested in population studies. Each of them usually had an additional room there. So did students who received fellowships to work in the population area and their fellowships were usually handled by the Center. The Center was the home for research efforts and was often characterized by its piles of questionnaires, its boxes of punched cards, its computing equipment, and its seminar room. Often the latter was employed for course work seminars and other teaching even though these were officially courses of a department which might be physically located elsewhere. Therefore, the Foundation grants were largely to fund secretaries, typewriters, accommodation (though this was sometimes provided free by the university), small libraries, core money which could be used to buy some time for faculty members off lecturing, some travel expenses to the Third World, and student fellowships. The Centers did not in any sense organize the faculty, as was made clear by Ronald Freedman in a statement to the Foundation. 'The Center as such has no program of research. The studies carried out by members of the professional staff and doctoral candidates reflect their individual interests. The Center seeks only to provide a setting within which they can work effectively on problems of their own choosing.' University administrations had no problems in receiving funds for Centers because they were not accepting any permanent commitment, or indeed any commitment beyond the funding period of two or three years.

Why, then, did the Population Centers change the nature of population teaching in many of America's most prestigious universities and thereby make the United States the major locus of population studies? Part of the answer lies in the short-term commitments provided by the Centers when they accepted fellowship moneys. This commitment was that much of the money would be spent on Third World students and a considerable part of the balance on American students with Third World interests. The provision of fellowships was part of a process whereby the support of American students in graduate studies was changing. The prewar situation had been that a department enrolled two or three outstanding students each year and arranged that they might support themselves as teaching assistants or more rarely as research assistants. This system was first partly transformed by government support for graduate students under the G.1. Bill of Rights after the War. Nevertheless, by 1960 major government support schemes for other students had not yet been fully developed and fellowships in the population field had a major impact on sociology departments. The first fellowships had been awarded to Princeton University's Office of Population Research by the Milbank Memorial Fund as early as 1937, when John Durand took the original fellowship, to be followed the next year by Ansley Coale and George Stolnitz. All these three and most students who have followed have stated that their original interests were in sociology or in economics or some other field and that they accepted a population element in their education in return for the financial support. Most stayed and enjoyed their new interests, but this pattern persisted at least until it was modified by popular enthusiasms about controlling fertility and protecting the environment in the 1960s and by the growth in the Third World of job opportunities in the field. There may be no other way of creating a new field in a short time. University departments felt an obvious moral commitment to provide additional courses once major funding had been accepted. This was not a difficult decision as the very existence of the students created a real demand and the fees paid by their fellowships helped to defray the cost of hiring lecturers. Once a Population Center and a program were established not all students were supported by the fellowship funds built into the grant. Others arrived from the Third World on Population Council Fellowships or on a variety of United Nations support, including WHO traineeships. Later, AID was to provide much of the money. Students from America and other industrialized countries were still occasionally supported by the older university financial arrangements.

A major mechanism for developing the program was the fact that the applicant for the funds was usually the head of the department most closely concerned and was often the director of the Center as well. He had usually consulted at least some of his colleagues, the Dean of the School, and the President of the University either before making his first move, or before agreeing to the acceptance of the Foundation grant. Nowhere were plans for whole programs drawn up but rather courses were suggested one at a time, employing the argument that they were also of value to the department as a whole. In fact in departments of sociology surprisingly few new courses were added. Even the most famous programs, such as that at Michigan, owed more of their Third World flavor to the origins and interests of their students, to the nature of the dissertations and to the publications of some members of the faculty than they did to the teaching programs.

The first three programs, and many that followed in the social sciences, had their major links to departments of sociology. In global terms this has had a major impact on the field. In other countries population interests had been more the concern of statisticians, economists, and geographers. Admittedly, the importance of migration studies in America had been influential in bringing sociologists to population interests. Nevertheless, Harkavy's action in turning first to sociology departments was to have a major and continuing influence on the population field in the United States and beyond.

Most population students took pre-existing courses such as those on the sociology of the family and survey research methodology as well as new courses. The existence of the Centers and their Ford Foundation link often meant that better persons were applying for departmental positions in the population field than in other fields and they were easily appointed. They were often attracted by relatively light teaching loads because the Center bought off part of their teaching loads, by the fact that the Center's reputation meant that research funds were easier to obtain, and by the travel money and contact with overseas countries that the Center provided. Some appointees came to the Centers as essentially researchers on soft money but contributed some teaching.

The strong link with sociology departments rather than with those of economics (Yale is something of an exception here) has continued to worry both foundations and universities. Princeton's Office of Population Research and Michigan's Population Studies Center have repeatedly sought funding and made appointments in order to provide a sounder basis for economic demography but the field has not been adequately institutionalized, perhaps because of its difficulty. However, by the early 1980s the University of Michigan had three economic demographers on its faculty and an increasing number of students in the field.

The potential impermanence of Centers made them easier to establish but may render them ephemeral. They may have only a very loose control over even one other department, as has been the case for years at the University of Pennsylvania. Clearly the question arises as to why there had been no concerted movement to establish departments of demography because there is a clear recognition in universities that only departments can institutionalize a discipline or a field. One reason is that most American demographers never cease to be sociologists and were themselves suspicious of the claim of demography to be a graduate field in its own right. Many of our respondents pointed to the collapse of the Department of Demography in the University of California at Berkeley as evidence that demography on its own was not viable but this evidence seems to be tenuous and based on a very specific situation. The University of Pennsylvania created a Master's Degree in Demography but this seems to have been at least partly an assurance to the University that they did not have to imply to all students that the fact of entry to the graduate program implied an acceptance that they were probably of doctoral caliber. Most of the programs drew little attention to the fact that most Third World students were accepted for terminal Master's degrees and that most Western students, if accepted at all, were assumed to be going through to the doctorate (as did some Third World students, as, for example, in the Ph.D. in Sociology at Pennsylvania).

As the programs expanded, fewer of their senior faculty worked on fundamental Third World research than has commonly been supposed. Even at the Population Studies Center at Michigan, involvement did not proceed beyond the Freedmans, Albert Hermalin, and David Goldberg (and in the 1970s John Knodel). In other programs there were senior faculty who had a great deal of contact with the Third World, such as Philip Hauser of Chicago and Vincent

Whitney of Pennsylvania, but they did not reside and research in developing countries. Those who did do so were usually doctoral or post-doctoral students engaged for a specific project. These projects were usually funded from sources other than the Ford Foundation; for instance, Michigan's work in Taiwan was financed successively by the Population Council and by NICHD.

In the 1960s the Population Centers were relatively affluent and were often remarkably independent within the universities in terms of the decisions they made. The money allowed them to bring in well-known demographers, as, for instance, with Chicago bringing in Nathan Keyfitz. It allowed many programs to create a critical mass of demographers. Although Princeton produced few demographers their production was almost entirely for university employment and in this way they continued to have a very significant influence on the developing programs. However, Chicago to some degree produced Michigan and Michigan staffed the University of Wisconsin while some Chicago demographers went directly to the University of Wisconsin.

In due course the American programs were strengthened by overseas links, such as the ones that Chicago forged with Ford Foundation help with the University of the Philippines, and as Michigan and Brown University demographers had with Chulalongkorn University, Bangkok, with the help of the Population Council. What remains remarkable is the relatively weak link between the activities of the Ford Foundation in the population field and those of the United Nations Population Division, a much weaker link than the Population Council has had with the United Nations.

In the interplay between Harkavy and the various programs, and in the context of changing public opinion, there is a marked change over time in the stated objectives of the programs.

The first application was that from the Population Studies Center of the University of Pennsylvania, a Center which had existed before Ford funding. Indeed the Ford Foundation substantially cut the original application for $1,218,000 to a five-year grant of $200,000, partly on the grounds that the Center had already received a grant of $175,000 from the Foundation for urban migration research. The emphasis in the application was on fellowships, with almost 60 percent of the original application being in this category. Very little overseas travel was envisaged but a substantial amount was intended for use in three conferences. The major emphasis was only on the Center providing a good demographic training for foreign and American students. The original application stated that the general purpose was to develop a Center which could provide rigorous and systematic training in demography for population specialists, social scientists, medical and public health workers, planners, and qualified government officials. The training would be available at both the doctoral and post-doctoral levels and would contribute indirectly to the solution of pressing current problems of fertility, mortality, migration, and population growth. American doctoral students would combine core work in population with interdisciplinary training in economic development, regional studies, political science, or urban planning. Doctoral students might be required to take the core demographic courses but to supplement these and their research with additional courses in such areas as statistics or survey methods.

Three points were very clear and were adhered to for a number of years. The first is that Pennsylvania did not intend to downgrade its earlier emphases on migration, urbanization, and the labor force in return for a major focus on fertility and fertility control in developing countries. The second is that there was no intention at that time that the program would plan a major involvement with one or more overseas countries. The third was that formal demography would be at the heart of the curriculum and would be the criterion of standards. The application slightly defensively emphasized the belief that the program could provide the needed emphasis on underdeveloped areas through full course and seminar coverage, through using these areas as the focus for research projects and dissertations, and through some American trainees going to the areas on fellowships to study and write at first hand.

It is probably fair to say that the Ford Foundation input changed the University of Pennsylvania less than any other major program. This is probably partly why the grant was limited to $40,000 a year in the first five years, $37,500 in the following five years, and $40,000 after that. It was to be the mid-1970s before the program developed an area speciality, Africa, and then with Rockefeller Foundation support, and the 1980s before Etienne van de Walle returned to field research there, and then in the area of mortality. Yet, with regard to teaching, Pennsylvania took in more Third World students, both as measured by numbers and as a fraction of the whole, than any other social science program. They also presented the greatest number and range of courses across the full demographic spectrum. Unlike Princeton, they assumed that a substantial proportion of their students were not proceeding to university positions. There was a strong sense of there being a community of students although the atmosphere was probably not quite as earnest as at Michigan. Often there were forty to fifty students in the Center's programs at any one time. The major contrasts with the program at Michigan were the lack of a faculty research program on an overseas country and the related absence of an apprenticeship or intern program whereby students participated in the analysis of data collected as part of the Center's research program.

In the early 1960s, Pennsylvania developed a Master's Degree in Demography and in the late 1960s a doctorate. The price was the separation of the Population Studies Center and the Graduate Group in Demography from the Department of Sociology or any other department. Later, when no head of department belonged to the Center this was to mean that budgetary relations with the university had to be negotiated at second hand.

The second application was from the University of Michigan at Ann Arbor. So close were the objectives of the Michigan program and those of the early Ford Foundation population program to be that it was to prove difficult to determine where leadership lay. Michigan told the Foundation in March 1961 that it wished to create a University of Michigan Population Center (it was actually to become The Population Studies Center) aiming: (a) to increase the number of American and foreign students trained to do research on population problems and to teach others to do so; (b) to help to build indigenous training and research programs in India or other underdeveloped areas; and (c) to foster sound research by graduate staff and students to increase the body of reliable knowledge in the population field. This program was so appealing that it received almost $100,000 a year for the first four years, while thereafter the demographic component of a broader university program received around $250,000 a year.

The program failed to make the necessary links with India, but by the end of 1960 Ronald Freedman had received the help of Notestein, Kirk, and Balfour of the Population Council in making contacts with the Taiwan Population Studies Center (later the Taiwan Institute of Family Planning) and the Taiwan Ministry of Health. This led to a major program in collaboration with the Taiwanese which both in itself and one aspect of it, the Taichung experiment,[159] has become a landmark in the demographic study of developing countries.[160] From 1964 there was a link with the records of a very large maternity hospital in Hong Kong and with the Chinese University of Hong Kong, and from later in the same year with the Malaysian Family Planning Program and a fertility and family planning survey of West Malaysia.[161] Early in these developments, Freedman located John Takeshita teaching on the American West Coast but with a dissertation from the University of Michigan.

None of this work meant having many Michigan students abroad, certainly not as many as had been originally hoped.

Students had their main contact with Asian data from data banks and seminars in Ann Arbor. Most students had contact with these data by working as apprentices for twelve hours per week on faculty research projects. Some also used the material for dissertations. This pattern became something of a model to be aimed at but never worked as well anywhere else as at Michigan.

The Ford Foundation did not finance the work in Taiwan which was supported first by the Population Council and later by NICHD. Nor did Michigan faculty work there for long periods. They helped to develop the projects which were largely carried through by their collaborators.

By 1968 the Population Studies Center had thirty-seven graduate students. There was said to be an air of great earnestness. To a greater extent than the University of Pennsylvania, and indeed, most other demographic programs, the Michigan Population Studies Center took an interest in observing and measuring the impact of family planning programs and this was regarded favorably not only by the Ford Foundation but by other foundations and technical aid organizations as well.

By 1964 there were plans afoot for a vast university-wide population umbrella covering three Population Centers, one in social sciences, one in public health, and one in the biomedical area. The chief architect was Moye Freymann, then a staff member, who served as a consultant, while, within the University, the lead was taken by Myron Wegman, Dean of the School of Public Health. By this time statements about the need for intervention in the Third World were much more outspoken:

The structure and growth of human population affects almost every aspect of society. Basic scientific and urgent practical problems alike require increased basic knowledge about population and the development of the skills to apply that knowledge. For example, recent rates of population growth are recognized as posing as critical and fundamental problems of adaption as any facing the human race.

Since rational analysis and plans to meet these problems are among the great challenges of our time, it is proposed to correlate, expand, and strengthen existing efforts at The University of Michigan in a coordinated, tripartite University of Michigan Population Program.

This plan secured $7,249,320 for the next twelve years and probably represents the high point of the Foundation's university population planning. The splendid vision faded. The social science and public health centers did not cooperate closely although the former provided service teaching courses in demography for the latter. The biomedical center withered. Wegman had attempted to persuade Freymann to become head of population work in the School of Public Health and to keep an interest in the whole university-wide program, but Freymann replied that he was more attracted by the alternative possibility of going to the University of North Carolina at Chapel Hill where he would have a 'completely clean sheet.'

In terms of the direct impact on the Third World situation, the Michigan program had a more measurable impact than any other and some of the decisions of the Taiwan family planning program can be shown to have emerged straight from the collaborative projects. The Taichung Project was influential not only in Taiwan but also in the development of a family planning program in South Korea.[162]

Over two years elapsed from March 1961 until, in mid-1963, the two Population Centers of the University of Chicago's Sociology Department applied jointly for funding. Both Centers were in existence before Foundation funding and indeed before the Foundation directly entered the population field. Philip Hauser's Population Research and Training Center was a traditional demography program with a considerable interest in labor force analysis. Donald Bogue's Community and Family Study Center was an unusual type of center for a sociology department and resembled in some ways the Centers which were later to be established in schools of public health. It had a strong interest in family planning programs and the focus of that interest lay in their effective communication.

The relations between the two Centers should be briefly explored because the tensions were similar to those that were to develop between the public health and sociology programs at the University of Michigan, and between those of different disciplines at the University of North Carolina and elsewhere. Although these difficulties were usually interpreted in terms of personality it is clear that they were largely products of the situation. The basic argument was between those who saw the social scientist as a neutral observer and those who believed that knowledge should be employed to change history for the better. There were sub-themes of course. One accusation was that the activist lost his objectivity and emphasized some findings while dismissing others as being of little significance or even as being best left unstated. Another was the charge of soft science and of low standards in both research experiment and teaching and testing rigor. A third was the possibility of error in deciding what was the better future for mankind. Against this lay the defense that economists had never thought that their objectivity was imperiled by entering on to the world stage and indeed regarded this as the only genuine type of social science experiment. They argued that the more traditional type of demography program was in danger of concentrating on matters of past or marginal importance and of losing sight of the substance because of preoccupation with the technique. Such strains had already emerged in Chicago in the early 1960s and it is claimed that this was the main reason that the joint proposal for funding, which the Ford Foundation preferred, could not be put forward until 1963. Subsequently, the Foundation was to accept separate proposals.

There does seem to be agreement that the graduate degrees awarded to those Sociology Department students attached to the Community and Family Studies Center were the product of rigorous dissertations. The course work was that of the

Sociology Department. However, the more unusual activity of the Center was its summer schools in family planning communications and related areas which drew into Chicago family planning workers from around the world, together with teachers with unusual experience and sometimes unusual credentials. There were also close relations with family planning activities in Chicago. The courses were run with great vigor by Donald and Elizabeth Bogue, starting in 1961 first with Population Council and then with Rockefeller Foundation funding before the Ford Foundation took over in 1963. It might be noted here that there is considerable evidence that these courses had a substantial impact around the world.

The joint Chicago application of 1963 was a good deal less cautious than the 1961 applications in specifying the need.

> Economic development cannot be achieved unless aggregate output increases more rapidly than total population. . . . Social science research is needed to learn more about how to increase motivation and incentive for the regulation of family size. Natural science research is needed to learn more about human reproduction so that more effective methods for controlling fertility may be developed. . . . The time to mount a major program of technical demographic assistance to help the nations with developing economies to lower their fertility is now at hand.

Philip Hauser envisaged the Population Research and Training Center providing a demographic service for developing economies. The aims would include the expansion of research and training in demography, and work in developing countries to improve basic demographic data, the furthering of demographic analysis and the development of population policy. Donald Bogue envisaged the Community and Family Studies Center training people from developing countries to work on their own countries' problems, using areas of rapid population growth in the United States as high fertility laboratories for research and training, and emphasizing practical experience in laboratory, workshop, and field observation sessions. He set the following specific goals:

(a) To establish a training facility equipped to train up quickly, but to a high level of competence, experts in communication and adult education especially experienced in family planning motivation, with trainees primarily from high birth-rate nations.
(b) To assemble a core staff capable of lending expert assistance in setting up or improving family planning programs anywhere in the world.
(c) To experiment with a wide variety of ideas and programs for inducing lower fertility.
(d) To test, compare, and evaluate family planning programs throughout the world.
(e) To help extend family planning training and research to Latin America and Africa.

In October, 1963 the Foundation made a grant to the University of Chicago of $700,000, half for each Center. In fact the Population Research and Training Center spent $25,000 less than budgeted and the Community and Family Studies Center almost $25,000 more, so that in January 1970 the University of Chicago returned a balance of $58.50 to the Foundation.

However, the Community and Family Studies Center secured another grant in 1966 from the Foundation and in total between 1963 and the final grant in 1974 received over $2 million while the Population Research and Training Center received almost $1,250,000.

In the second application Donald Bogue set out his aim as 'to continue with expansion in scope, a program of making a social science contribution to the international drive to reduce population growth.' He promised 'to review systematically the theories, researches and methodologies of sociology and social psychology and to devise experiments whereby these may be applied directly to family planning action programs in order to test their applicability.' By the late 1960s the emphasis was on involvement overseas with family planning programs and research, which led after 1971 to the phasing out of the summer schools and the holding of international workshops in such cities as Seoul, Santiago, and Lagos.

The Population Research and Training Center pointed to success in consolidating its program and in providing basic demography training courses for the students of both Centers. Philip Hauser's travels were the main instrument for linking the program with the Third World. He participated in 1963 with Oscar Harkavy and Dudley Kirk in an exploratory mission to Southeast Asia and subsequently assisted with the development of the Population Program at the University of the Philippines and with the creation in Southeast Asia and Chicago of the Organization of Demographic Associates. In addition to the usual demographic courses, the University of Chicago offered courses on the labor force and population and economic development as well as another on population in Southeast Asia. The Population Research and Training Center endeavored to create a research apprenticeship system for students but this did not develop to the extent of that in Michigan because of the lack of an overseas research laboratory equivalent to Taiwan.

A major innovation was the funding of a Master's program at the London School of Economics through David Glass. Negotiations began in late 1963 and resulted in a five-year grant of $240,000 in February 1964. Harkavy had described the resource base for the development of training as being the industrialized world, but the substantial support for the LSE program was a unique involvement outside the United States (with the exception of a three-year supplementary grant to the Department of Demography, Australian National University, from 1976, for a Master's program which was primarily supported by the University and the Australian Government).

The London School of Economics and Political Science

was founded as an independent institution but was subsequently brought into the loose confederation of the University of London. Its tradition of population studies had
been established after the First World War by Alexander
Carr-Saunders who later headed LSE. Names associated
with the institution had included Robert Kuczynski, Lancelot
Hogben—who had been Professor of Social Biology (and
who was married to Enid Charles)—and Glass who had
entered demography as a research assistant for Carr-Saunders's
1936 book, *World Population*. Glass had long provided
a course on demography which was taken by both undergraduate and graduate students. Some students did Masters
or doctoral degrees on population themes, usually formally
in the Department of Statistics supervised by Norman Carrier
or John Hajnal or in the Department of Sociology, supervised
by Glass.

After the Second World War, in preparation for Independence, the University of London developed university colleges
in the West Indies, Ghana, Nigeria (at Ibadan), Uganda
(Makerere), Sudan (Khartoum), and later in Kenya
(Nairobi).[163] By the beginning of the 1960s the University
of the West Indies and the University of Ghana, the latter
with Population Council support, had chosen to take the
LSE demography papers for the BA/BSc degree. Thus, by
1963, there was a demand from African students at the
University of Ghana and from Asian Commonwealth students
for admission to LSE for continued work in demography of
a type that was not easily fully met by the existing structure.
Glass proposed to Harkavy the development of both Master's
and doctoral courses. Although these were courses at LSE,
the Ford Foundation actually made out the grant to a
private association, the Population Investigation Committee,
which published *Population Studies* and which had a membership which blended older British interests in both population
and eugenics. There is no doubt that Glass welcomed this
degree of independence which allowed him to personally
appoint the teaching staff.

The grant mostly provided for teaching and gave some support to *Population Studies* which was the flagship of demography journals in the English-speaking world. There was little relation between faculty teaching and Third World research although one faculty member took leave to join University of Michigan researchers in the West Malaysian Fertility Survey. During the first ten years of the program there were 133 students, of whom seventy-nine were from developing countries, including a significant proportion from Africa. In total the program was funded to the extent of $680,000.

The LSE Master's program differed from the American programs in several ways. There was no Population Studies Center and the funds were used almost entirely to support students and teaching. Some existing LSE staff such as Glass gave lectures but there was not a reciprocal contribution by LSE. Those Master's graduates who wished to go on to a doctorate normally returned first to their own countries to teach. If they managed to undertake research while doing this they could later apply to return to London with their research data to undertake a doctorate by thesis. This was one of the factors in explaining the almost complete return of graduates to positions in their own countries.

The Ford Foundation expands its population activities

This first era of establishing teaching programs in population in the developed world, employing Foundation funds and a single Foundation Officer, was changed, partly because of its own success, with the announcement of the establishment of a Ford Foundation Population Program in late 1963 and with the appointment in February 1964 of Lyle Saunders, the first new staff member additional to Harkavy.

The situation in early 1964 was very different from late 1959. The battle for placing Third World family planning on the public agenda was slowly being won. In July 1963 the Senate Foreign Relations Committee approved an amendment to the Foreign Aid Bill devoting funds specifically to cooperating countries in carrying out programs of population control. The following month President Kennedy approved $500,000 to be given to WHO for research into human reproduction. By the end of the year it was clear that President Johnson's Administration would strongly support aid to Third World family planning programs.

In 1959 there were only two national family planning programs, that which had begun in 1952 in India and the recently announced program in Pakistan. By the end of 1963 these were both better established and showing some signs of success and had been joined by Taiwan, Korea, and Tunisia. Furthermore, there was evidence that organized family planning had probably contributed to declines in fertility in Singapore, Hong Kong, and Taichung (Taiwan), as well as evidence of fertility decline owing much to family planning in Puerto Rico and such parts of the Caribbean as Jamaica and Trinidad.

Perhaps most important was the fact that apparently

satisfactory methods for controlling Third World fertility were beginning to emerge. The position in 1959 had not been very different from the despairing situation that Notestein had described for China in the report on the 1948 mission to the Far East. The situation by the end of 1963 was immensely different. The pill had been news in the West from 1960 when it began to become generally available. It was still far too expensive for mass use in the Third World but there were frequent forecasts that the situation would change radically within a few years. In October, 1963 Christopher Tietze had told an IPPF seminar of the emergence of three types of IUD and from the beginning it was felt that cost was no problem with these devices. If anything, the possibility of problems with both forms of contraceptives was understated and they appeared to have joined sterilization, and abortion where acceptable, to provide a wide range of suitable family planning methods.

The appearance of the pill had another quite dramatic effect on the population debate in that its nature and the possibility of its acceptance as a licit method so divided the Catholic Church that there was never again to be a politically important Catholic opposition to the use of technical aid funds to support either biomedical research into human reproduction or Third World family planning programs. Later in 1964 the Vatican Commission began its inquiry into oral contraception that was to last over two years.

The Ford Foundation Population Program was to have nineteen appointments altogether, the last being in February 1977, and the Program, as a separate administrative entity, being finally phased out in September, 1983. Significantly, the next appointments after Saunders were a biomedical appointee, Anna Southam, in August, 1965, and an appointee essentially to overseas biomedical and family planning work, Gordon Perkin, in October 1966. They were followed by more social scientists, Davidson Gwatkin and Lenni Kangas in October, 1967, the former heading for Africa and the latter for India. Robert McLaughlan followed in 1968 and a communications expert, William Sweeney, joined in February, 1969. The demographers were represented by Edwin Driver for sixteen months from June, 1969, while James Bausch joined in September, 1969, spending a substantial time in Indonesia. Michael Teitelbaum arrived in 1970 and was to spend nine of the next dozen years with the group. Ozzie Simmons followed in 1971 spending five of the next ten years with the program and the balance of the time with the Foundation's regional offices overseas.

The way that the Population Program worked was determined largely by the Foundation's structure which gave great independence to Regional Offices and very substantial power to Regional Representatives. From 1959, when Harkavy was given a mandate to work in the population field, any Regional Representative could fund projects in this area. From late 1963, when the Population Program came into existence, they were largely obliged to have at least some population interests and most showed considerable enthusiasm for such activities. With the appointment in 1966 of David Bell as Vice President in charge of the new International Division there was a high-ranking officer who regarded population as a specific part of his duties.

It is not easy to work out in retrospect just how the program functioned and why its expenditure grew so rapidly. Clearly, one of the mechanisms was the writing of internal papers for consideration within the Foundation; Harkavy did a great deal of this. The Population Program very actively participated in the most important of the Foundation's processes for central coordination, the regular meetings of Regional Representatives with selected Head Office staff which were usually held in Europe. During the 1960s population reports became an important part of the agenda and a 1967 meeting at Lake Como also included outsiders from the Population Council and further afield. Ronald Freedman was able to tell that meeting that it could now be shown that interventionist policies had considerably reduced fertility levels in South Korea and Taiwan as well as Singapore and

Hong Kong. In addition, the Regional Offices were increasingly visited by staff members of the Population Program and from 1966 there were appointments, starting with Gordon Perkin, of staff who would spend most of their time attached to overseas offices.

Most of the population expenditure on the Third World was not budgeted out of the New York Office but was decided upon by the Regional Offices and included in their budgets. In effect, they increasingly frequently selected and financially supported Population Program personnel to spend considerable periods with them on specific projects. For instance, when in the late 1960s Haldore Hanson, the Foundation Representative for West Africa, decided to pursue a vigorous population program, he had Davidson Gwatkin attached to the Lagos post for two years and William Sweeney there for two periods each of several months working on media matters. Inevitably, such persons, when attached to Regional Offices, advised on budgeting matters. Similarly, in Turkey Eugene Northrop brought Frederic Shorter into the population field after he was attached to the Ankara Office as a Middle East expert and arranged for his association with university programs.

As was true with other substantive programs in the Foundation's International Division, each country or regional Representative made his own staff appointments, including population specialists, and was responsible for all grants in his territory which were funded out of his regional budget. The Population Program—later called the Population Office—was administratively unique in that it was the only substantive office in the hierarchy of the International Division in New York (the other offices dividing the world geographically). Perhaps the program's major impact on Foundation employees in other parts of the world was achieved through a series of five international meetings held every few years, bringing together Foundation people from New York and overseas, especially the regional Representatives, often with outside experts in order to discuss strategy and specific topics such as management, communications and links with the social sciences. After the 1967 meeting at Lake Como, other meetings were held in Rome, Elsinor, Cali and Bangkok. The creation of a community of interest was achieved because some, but not all, of the population specialists in the field office had previously worked in the New York Program. They included Gwatkin, McLaughlin, Perkin, Saunders and Simmons. A more continuing impact was that provided by the frequent travel of the New York Program personnel to the field to interact with Foundation colleagues on general strategy and specific grants.

There is widespread agreement among the recipients that the money received in the early 1960s from the Foundation for population work had fewer strings than money from other sources or than more recent grants from the Foundation's Population Program. Equally unanimously, they believed that these early flexible grants were the most efficient form of funding and that their existence permitted the rapid growth of new types of teaching programs. It might be noted that the Foundation had ample money at that time, a situation which did not change appreciably until investments on the stock market proved unsatisfactory toward the end of the decade. As a source of funds the Foundation was the giant until various governmental agencies entered the field in the second half of the decade. By the mid-1960s the Foundation's Population Program was spending massively on reproductive biology and half of all its population funds were ultimately spent in this way.

The Public Health Programs

By 1963 family planning programs were spreading in the Third World. In 1959, when the first program in India had needed training for its personnel, Freymann had written not to demographers but to public health schools to explore whether appropriate courses could be developed. This initiative was resumed in 1963.

The first School of Hygiene and Public Health in the world had been established at Johns Hopkins University in 1918. The Rockefeller Foundation had been pouring money into the University's Medical School since 1913 and had also played the major funding role in setting up the School of Public Health, as it was also to do at Harvard from 1921. These schools of public health emerged partly from the Rockefeller Foundation's concern with campaigns in tropical countries against infectious diseases and never wholly lost their international interests.[164] They were always institutions which put together courses of different types for health workers who had often to be generalists and who needed an understanding of society. In later years they frequently worked on specific projects with government and other grants and depended on a bigger proportion of short-term earmarked funds than did other university schools. They were still developing after the Second World War when massive money from governments and international organizations became available in the health field. Some of their staff members who had worked in densely settled poor countries had begun to take an interest in population control during the 1950s and by 1960 a few were arguing that high fertility could be regarded as an epidemiological problem.

From 1963, the Foundation's Population Program began to take an interest in developing population programs in these schools, beginning with Johns Hopkins and Harvard. Looking retrospectively over all these programs, certain generalizations can be attempted.

The faculty had more experience in Third World countries than did those in social science programs. On the other hand, many of them had much less university experience. Almost uniquely, it was sometimes possible to attain a full professorship or to head a program without substantial university experience. This meant that there was often a lack of understanding of university attitudes, traditions, and procedures. Sometimes tactless institutional mistakes were unwittingly made. Because of their experience outside the university world, some of those involved in the public health programs tended to regard universities as a means to an end, as a tool for controlling runaway global population growth. Inevitably, they clashed with those who regarded universities as the central but fragile repository for truth and the intellectual tradition of civilization. To the latter, involvement and activism often appeared to be treason to institutions and ways of life that alone would make the world worth saving.

Thus, it was not a case of a clash between good and evil but between two goods and between people with different experiences, perspectives, and priorities. The theme was the fundamental one of Greek tragedy and often contained the same ironic elements. In each institution the clash was blamed upon specific individuals but the widespread nature of these tensions clearly shows that fundamental problems lay underneath. Versions of the clash could take place solely within the social sciences, as occurred between the two Population Centers of Chicago's Sociology Department, or between social science and public health programs, as in the University of California at Berkeley or as at Harvard where the major social science and economics departments remain defensively neutral. However, the greatest tensions could be found within public health programs and led to explosions of the kind that occurred at North Carolina in 1974 and in the Michigan School of Public Health in 1977.

Future university historians may well adopt a more sanguine long-term perspective than did participants and may regard the whole process as one which allowed the universities to play an important and unusual role during a decisive period, while ultimately retaining everything that they held dear. The truth is, in fact, somewhat more complex than this. Activism in the Third World in a gigantic experiment allowed some of the participants to be social science researchers in a way that can hardly fail to benefit academic understanding of social change in important areas remote from the metropolitan universities.

A full understanding of these programs demands some appreciation of what they wanted to do. In their first applications, Harvard cautiously laid stress on the advancement of knowledge. However, Johns Hopkins referred to the need 'to prepare administrators, demographers, physiologists and social scientists for careers in this area [i.e. national family planning programs].' In an internal memorandum the Ford Foundation identified the situation even more specifically as a

> need for 125–150 specialists in family planning, from overseas and the United States, to train in U.S. schools of public health to equip them for leadership roles in family planning work. . . . Family planning should be established as a functional field of public health on equal footing with such traditional areas as epidemiology and environmental sanitation.

The mark of programs in the schools of public health was activism. Most tried to have links with overseas programs and it was usually commented that the heads of the programs travelled a great deal. Most of the faculty were said to have less impressive publication lists than in social science programs; some of the faculty retorted that long publication lists were not what they were about and that they had resisted this form of academic disease. The public health students usually had more varied backgrounds than those in social science, many having lived overseas and perhaps a majority of the American students having worked at some time with an action-orientated service program. It was said that they had a strong group spirit and less earnest devotion to purely academic ideals and success than most students in the social sciences. Part of the reason was that the public health population programs concentrated on the M.P.H. degree or, for those focussing mostly on demography, on the M.Sc. Often doctoral programs were developed only after some years and even then only for a minority. Neither the teachers nor the students themselves regarded most students as being trained to become researchers.

There were sometimes strains within the schools of public health and the wider medical academic fraternity about the population programs. These strains seem to have been of four types. Firstly, although schools of public health have been accustomed to unorthodox disciplines, there was some reaction to the fact that the majority of population program faculty often did not come from the health field at all. Secondly, there was a dwindling core who maintained that high fertility was not a health matter. Thirdly, there was sometimes a jealously of the funds available to population programs and occasionally plotting to see if these resources could be made available to other parts of the schools. Fourthly, there have been some accusations that enthusiasm has at times been a substitute for scientific standards.

The programs were not always certain about the exact nature of the products they were turning out but the most common description was of family planning administrators, especially for Third World national family planning programs. By the early 1970s, students, especially American students, were worrying about a decline in potential overseas jobs. The programs by this time, as in the social sciences in general, were characterized by a rising proportion of female students. Many of the faculty were wondering whether the demand for Third World family planning administrators was likely to be trivial compared with the demand for health administrators in the developed world.

The Johns Hopkins School of Hygiene and Public Health had begun to move into the population field as early as 1958. Paul Harper had worked in the Pacific in public health during the Second World War, visiting Japan afterwards and taking an interest in the move towards abortion. By 1953 he had considerable contact with the family planning movement in Baltimore. In 1958 Notestein and Balfour, representing the Population Council and the Rockefeller Foundation respectively, came to Baltimore to ask whether Harper would organize a population course essentially for Americans because institutions working in the population field were beginning to need overseas consultants. They said that the Rockefeller Foundation would fund the course and a grant was received for this purpose. Shortly afterwards, arguing that the receipt of the grant and the teaching of the course necessitated a greater commitment, Balfour persuaded Harper to go on a mission to Pakistan to see what could be done to help the new family planning program. Harper did so and recommended three demonstration family planning areas, two in West Pakistan and one in East Pakistan. These were established, partly with Population Council funding, with Berkeley involvement in the East and Johns Hopkins and Swedish participation in the West. As Johns Hopkins links with the Pakistan project strengthened, a need to expand training in Baltimore both for Americans and Pakistanis was felt but appeals to the Rockefeller Foundation for further funding were not successful. In 1963 Harper wrote to Harkavy about the problem and was encouraged to make a formal application which was lodged in March 1964, a month after the Harvard School of Public Health had made an application. Johns Hopkins proposed a Division of Population Dynamics, arguing that 'many informed persons believe that the need for controlling population growth is the world's most important problem, not even excepting the need to control atomic weapons.' They argued that public health programs had an unusual responsibility because of the role they had already played in reducing mortality and hence creating rapid population growth. They pointed out that they already had good courses but

> There has not been time for enough individual attention to students. There needs to be more emphasis on the sociologic and psychologic factors which motivate behavior. Two or more courses need to be added, one to focus on the problem of promoting family planning within the individual family and the local community, and one or more on the physiology of fertility regulation.

The purpose of the new Division of Population Dynamics would be 'to strengthen and to expand teaching and research in population and fertility regulation and to prepare administrators, demographers, physiologists, and social scientists for careers in this area.' The Foundation provided a grant of $800,000, using a formula based on the University's proven ability to raise funds: $200,000 outright; an additional $200,000 if matched 1 : 1; a further $200,000 if matched 2 : 1; and a final $200,000 if matched 3 : 1.

Perhaps the most notable aspect of the Johns Hopkins program is that it had fewer strains than any other population program in a school of public health. Its first head was not imported but was very much part of the pre-existing establishment of the school. Two other features must be noted. The first is the tripartite division between demography and related social sciences, family planning administration, and reproductive biology. Both mathematical demography and reproductive biology have aimed at higher levels of reseach-based teaching than has been the general case in schools of public health or than would be thought necessary or even desirable in most schools. The second point is that the research program had its strongest Third World links when funding first started. The connection with West Pakistan weakened after the Indo-Pakistan war of 1965 and disappeared in the 1970s. Under the headship of Henry Mosley, there were relations with the Cholera Research Laboratory in Dhaka (Dacca), but even then, and certainly under the third head, John Kantner, the greatest development of research was in the United States. Kantner and Melvin Zelnick carried out research on fertility among younger black and white females.

The program has been described as 'a major source of training of family planning operators and technical assistance to family planning programs.' The work was carried out within a Department of Population Dynamics which provided a one-year M.P.H. for administrators, preferably M.D.s, and a two-year demography-orientated M.Sc. By the early 1970s there were forty-two students, of whom twelve were doctoral candidates and over half came from developing countries. The program had a small but good population library but, because of the division of the Johns Hopkins campus, was on the other side of the city from the Arts and Sciences Division where the broader range of social science books were to be found.

However, a prior application was received from the Harvard School of Public Health although this was not funded until July 1964. The central figure in establishing the Harvard program was John Synder who had been a microbiologist with the malaria program in Egypt during the Second World War when he became conscious of the problems of population growth in poor agrarian areas. However, Harvard and MIT began their main interest in population when John Gordon was asked to prepare a lecture on population for the 1952 International Conference on Tropical Health which led straight to the Khanna study with John Wyon (and later Carl Taylor), financed by the Rockefeller Foundation.[165] Snyder focussed his interest on population when he was asked to speak in a social issues series at Riverside Church, New York, in 1957. When he became Dean of the School of Public Health in 1959, he became drawn further into the field by having to raise funds for the Khanna study.

In February 1964 the School of Public Health lodged a funding application with the Ford Foundation to help to establish a Center for Population Studies for the whole university. It was argued that there was a need for concerted action to curb population growth.

> The populations of many areas of the world are increasing so rapidly that current efforts to improve economic and social conditions seem foredoomed to failure despite the expenditure of funds on a scale unprecedented in history. . . . The *immediate task* [their italics] confronting civilization is to achieve a sharp reduction in birth rates in many parts of the world. To participate in the accomplishment of this immediate task, the Harvard School of Public Health plans to establish a Center wherein research will be closely coordinated with fieldwork in order to obtain as rapidly as possible the knowledge necessary for the accomplishment of the immediate goals of society. . . . The *long-range objectives* of the Center are to develop comprehensive definitions of 'optimum population' in the broad context of human and economic resources, social needs, and scientific advances. The Center will also seek to assist the peoples of various regions and cultures to achieve their goals of optimum population.

Clearly, the application was prepared by the public health faculty as no social scientist would have spoken in the 1960s of fixed optimum populations.

The key to Snyder's strategy was the establishment of a Population Center which was needed at Harvard to bridge not only the distance between public health and social science disciplines but also the geographical distance between the campuses. The Population Center was accordingly established in Cambridge, miles across the Charles River from the Medical and Public Health Schools but close to the Departments of Sociology and Economics. Snyder also needed the Center and its funding to attract local endowments from wealthy families in the Boston area which he did with spectacular success, creating eight endowed chairs, which have proved to be the backbone of the program, defending it from changes in its nature or suggestions that funds might be otherwise deployed. There is nothing equivalent elsewhere in the population field and the achievement is a tribute to Snyder, the prestige of Harvard, and the old wealth of the Boston area. In some of this fundraising he was assisted by an old resident of the area, Clarence Gamble, who had been in the population field since 1922.

The Center was not so successful in attracting the social scientists of Harvard. It has always had a number of its own social scientists, some in the endowed chairs, but it has attracted no major commitment to population studies by either the Department of Sociology or the Department of Economics. The teaching program remains largely an operation of the Department of Population Sciences in the School of Public Health where some members of the Center for Population Studies also teach.

The Center obtained from the Foundation $250,000 in July, 1964 and a further $383,000 in July, 1967. However, a request for a major grant in 1972 did not succeed but was replaced instead by a $2 million grant from AID, the only untied grant of this kind given to a Population Center by AID. This was referred to AID by Harkavy and energetically pressed by Snyder. The first Director of the Population Center was Roger Revelle, who had been trained in oceanography, and who gave the very popular introductory course on Resources and Population which attracted large numbers of students from a wide range of disciplines. The endowed chairs included such areas as Population Policy and Population Ethics. They were employed to attract to Harvard such people as Harvey Leibenstein and Nathan Keyfitz. The Harvard program contained individuals such as Wyon, but, although there were attempts to extend work in Bangladesh, the overseas connections were never strong. All students took degrees within the Department of Population Sciences either as an M.P.H. or a D.Sc. in Population Sciences.

The attempts to constitute university-wide programs in population proceeded further later in 1964 when a meeting was held at the University of Michigan to discuss the possibility of establishing such a program based on three Population Centers, that already headed by Freedman and related to the Sociology and Economics Departments, a Center of Population Planning in the School of Public Health and a Biomedical Center for Research in Human Reproduction in the School of Medicine. President Harlan Hatcher was strongly behind the move. Moye Freymann, on study leave at the University from his post in India, designed courses for the future Center for Population Planning. The Trustees of the Ford Foundation granted $3 million for this purpose in December 1964 and noted that

> Recognition of the urgency of the world population problem and of the magnitude and variety of efforts needed to cope with it have contributed to a decision by a major university to commit itself to a long-range involvement in the wide spectrum of interests and actions needed for an adequate approach to the problem.

The University had affirmed in requesting the grant:

> The structure and growth of human populations affects almost every aspect of society. Basic scientific and urgent practical problems alike require increased basic knowledge about population and the development of the skills to apply that knowledge. For example, recent rates of population growth are recognized as posing as critical and fundamental problems of adaption as any facing the human race. Since rational analysis and plans to meet these problems are among the great challenges of our time, it is proposed to correlate, expand, and strengthen existing efforts at the University of Michigan in a co-ordinated, tripartite University of Michigan Population Program.

In fact the Biomedical Center never became fully established, and the Michigan program basically consisted of the other two Centers. Of the total 1964 grant the Center of Population Planning received $700,000 and in 1967 the

Foundation gave it another $1,500,000. At first only the M.P.H. and M.S. (i.e. M.Sc.) degrees were awarded but in the early 1970s the D.P.H. was also added after the establishment of a Department of Population Planning in late 1971. The course requirements for the M.S. remained fairly flexible because these were stipulated by the School of Graduate Studies rather than the School of Public Health. By 1972 there were thirty-nine students, twelve of them from developing countries, of whom twenty-eight were undertaking the M.P.H. degree, two the M.S., and nine the D.P.H. The last degree was replaced in 1975 by the Ph.D. when this was approved by the Graduate School.

The program concentrated on the development and evaluation of family planning programs. It aimed to produce family planning administrators rather than researchers. Much of the teaching suited to family planning administrators was presented not only for the usual degree students but also in summer course and spring half-term programs to which Third World family planning staff came on fellowships for a few months. Population psychology was introduced by the joint appointment of Lois Hoffman. The Center had stated its aims to the Foundation as the 'synthesis and application of knowledge from many sources,' and its strategy as being to 'combine elements of basic fields such as the social sciences and reproductive biology with those of administration and education to discover and teach better ways of promoting reproduction among human populations.' An only partly achieved aim was to 'build demographic and population content into the program of every appropriate student in the School of Public Health.'

Many of the original faculty appointees had overseas experience but for most these contacts tended to decline as the program developed. Perhaps a major reason was that five had their chief contact with India, which was increasingly reluctant to provide clearance for further field-work. John (Yuzuru) Takeshita had the only strong links with the Population Studies Center and he collaborated with Freedman on the Taiwan research.[166] George and Ruth Simmons collaborated in the early 1970s with the Kanpur Institute of Technology on a detailed and revealing study of the family planning program in rural Uttar Pradesh which unfortunately was not published for a decade.[167] Other contacts were made with the family planning programs in Nepal and Malaysia, in the latter case together with the Population Studies Center and the Ford Foundation.

Leslie Corsa arrived to direct the program in July 1965. He had been active in promoting family planning activities in the California Department of Health and had attracted the attention of Balfour when it was found necessary to provide Population Council funds for these activities to the University of California rather than to the California State Administration. From about 1976 financial cuts were made in the University by means of a program review process when funding from the Michigan State Government became tighter as the State's economy slowed down. Divisions developed within the Faculty of the Department of Population Planning along the now classical lines of family planning program or academic standard priorities and in March 1977 the Department of Family Planning was dissolved and the Center for Population Planning reconstituted. The new Head of the Center was a demographer, Yuzuru Takeshita, followed eighteen months later by Jason Finkle, a political scientist with experience in pre-war Vietnam and India (where he had served with the Foundation family planning staff) who had also made a study of the response of the United Nations system to global population growth. Debate occurred within and without the University, and Ford Foundation funding was halted. One positive achievement of the controversy was that the University offered a form of compensation by placing on University salaries some members of the Department who were previously supported on external funds. Faculty were placed in various Departments such as Maternal and Child Health but continued to teach the population programs as a degree course. Subsequently, review groups reported favorably and limited terminal Ford Foundation funding was resumed. That funding had been applied for 'to enhance the quality of research and training . . . as well as to correct certain weaknesses.' By this time student enrollment was a little over half the level in the early 1970s. There is evidence of a reversal of this trend in the early 1980s, attributed by Finkle to a success 'in effectively marrying the health and social sciences in a way not attempted by any other population training and research institute.' Large funding had been obtained which included a provision for sending graduates overseas for two-year internships, while the Center had made the largest single contribution to staffing the AID population program.

The desired university-wide program was finally achieved neither at Harvard nor Michigan but on the Chapel Hill Campus of the University of North Carolina. The Ford Foundation received a proposal from the University, the chief protagonist being Professor S. C. Jain, whose field was health administration, in August 1965, and the following month approved $800,000 for a three-to-five year period. The University requested Ford Foundation assistance in order to mobilize its full potential to meet world population problems and a broader education of its students and to allow the University to generate more permanent financial support. During the next decade the University's population activities on the campus and around the world would absorb $3.5 million from the Ford Foundation and $34 million from all sources.

As part of the total funding package Freymann arrived in 1966 as Director of the Carolina Population Center. The Center operated rather like a small foundation on the campus, negotiating with departments across the university about the funding needed to establish new courses or to recruit faculty or carry out research projects. Often the Center suggested specific names, such as Forrest Linder and Amos Hawley, and sometimes, as in the case of Stephen Polgar, brought faculty to the campus without the prior negotiation of Departmental attachment.

These activities were spectacularly successful. By the time of the 1966 application for an additional $700,000 of funding from the Foundation, it could be said that a population component existed in fifteen university departments. It was said that not only had population teaching spread widely but that

> Participating faculty have planned research into a wide spectrum of methodological and theoretical, as well as highly applied, problems related to fertility limitation. . . . The Population Center will create a reservoir of competent technical assistance personnel to meet various needs. It will emphasize assisting other universities in the developing world in order that they might handle the basic training and research needs of their own countries.

Much emphasis was placed both by the University and the Ford Foundation on the major effort which was to be directed toward the preparation of case studies, along the lines of business and public administration teaching cases, related to the administration of family planning programs throughout the world. It was believed that there was a great need for such studies for use in training programs in family planning both in the United States and abroad. It would probably be fair to say that these latter high expectations were not fully met, although the Popcase Project did produce a great deal of published material. By 1968 the Ford Foundation component of external funding was down to 22 percent and halved again within the next two years. By 1971 the Carolina Population Center had not only the Popcase Project but also the Population Dynamics Program (PDP) and POPLAB directed by Forrest Linder. PDP aimed at producing university-wide population programs, largely modeled on Chapel Hill, in universities around the world. The University of North Carolina was to provide faculty for periods and other technical assistance for longer duration, while training local faculty for these overseas programs at Chapel Hill. The program did not develop as widely as was originally intended but it took over the pre-existing Population Council-supported program at the University of Ghana and helped to establish new programs at the University of Bogota in Colombia, at Mahidol University in Bangkok, Thailand, and at the University of Shiraz, Teheran. The POPLAB program set up experimental projects, often employing dual record systems to improve the collection of fertility and mortality data, in a range of Third World countries, such as Morocco and Kenya.

Almost inevitably, the University began to experience divisions of attitudes about the extent to which university policies and programs were being decided from the Carolina Population Center. Its operations were on such a big scale that it was always possible to point to undesirable incidents here and there and in 1974 problems arose concerning the Shiraz program. More seriously, the inherent conflict about the aims of universities and the needs of the world surfaced and there was debate about the caliber of courses and some of the faculty appointments. There was also argument about the extent of departmental influence on the Population Center decision-making process. In 1974 Freymann was relieved of his Directorship of the Carolina Population Center, although he retained his chair in the Department of Public Health. The issues were complex and have been somewhat illuminated by legal wrangles over the following decade.

By the late 1970s, there were many fewer foreign students in population courses at the University of North Carolina than had been the case prior to 1974 but there is evidence that the numerical decline had begun as early as 1970. The Carolina Population Center, under J. Richard Udry, had become a model of academic respectability and the majority of its work was concentrated on the United States.

After 1965, the Ford Foundation's Population Program still had many important roles to play, including the continued provision of flexible support for University programs already begun and the taking of a new initiative in the form of supporting Third World programs. Yet, at least in the

United States, its unique and solitary role in the area of University population teaching was coming to an end. In good foundation fashion, Ford Foundation staff helped to achieve that end largely by promoting much greater Government involvement. To understand the population field after the mid-1960s, we must pause for a moment to examine both international events and changes within the United States during this period.

A turning-point, 1965–1967

The period from 1965 was, like the late 1950s, one of decisive change both within the United States and on the international scene. It is difficult not to interpret the rapidity of change as largely flowing from a decision in Washington at the Executive level and announced by President Lyndon Johnson in the State of the Union Message of January 4, 1965, his first after achieving a presidential electoral victory in his own right.

The United States Government had already moved its position significantly since the 1959 statement by President Eisenhower, 'I cannot imagine anything more emphatically a subject that is not a proper political or governmental activity. . . . This Government will not . . . as long as I am here, have a positive political doctrine in its program that has to do with this problem of birth control. That's not our business.' It was the business of the family and religion.[168] Change began in 1961 when President Kennedy, in a special message on foreign aid, said 'The magnitude of the problem is staggering, in Latin America, for example, population growth is already threatening to outpace economic growth. And in some parts of the continent living standards are actually declining . . . and the problems are no less serious or demanding in other developing parts of the world.' In December, 1962, the United States informed the United Nations General Assembly that it was concerned about population trends, that it would, upon request, find potential sources of information and assistance to deal with population problems and that there was a need for additional information. In January, 1963 the Department of Health, Education and Welfare released a survey which showed that research on reproduction and family planning was absorbing over

$8 million a year, of which approximately half came from Federal Government research funds. In July, 1963 the Senate Foreign Relations Committee approved an amendment to the Foreign Aid Bill devoting funds specifically to co-operating countries in carrying out programs of population control, and, in August, 1963, $500,000 was given to WHO for research into human reproduction. Nevertheless, massive American involvement really stems from President Johnson's statement on January 4, 1965 to Congress, 'I will see new ways to use our knowledge to help deal with the explosion in world population and the growing scarcity of world resources.'

To a considerable extent these changes were provoked by external events. Family planning programs were now in existence in India, Pakistan, South Korea, and Taiwan. Intensive private programs with government financial assistance also existed in Singapore and Hong Kong and it appeared that there was low-key governmental provision of services from about 1962. Several other countries were clearly moving to this situation and by the Conferences of August and September 1965 it was possible to add to the list Turkey, Malaysia, and Singapore with government programs, and Sri Lanka, Egypt, Chile, Honduras, and Mauritius with government support.

Substantial stimulus came from the International Conference on Family Planning Programs, which was held in Geneva in August, 1965, largely on the initiative of Berelson, now Vice President of the Population Council, with the sponsorship of the Ford Foundation and the Population Council, with additional support from the Rockefeller Foundation. Its *Proceedings*, a volume of 848 pages, was published the following year and distributed in very large numbers so that for some time it was the encyclopedic reference to the field.[169] There were 200 participants from thirty-six countries reporting either the existence of national family planning programs or movements towards them in at least twenty countries. Immediately afterwards, in August–September

1965, the United Nations and the International Union for the Scientific Study of Population cooperated in organizing the Second World Population Conference in Belgrade, attended by 2,000 delegates and yielding four volumes of *Proceedings.*[170]

During 1965, various American Government agencies were prodded by the Executive to produce plans for programs in the population field. Most internal American programs would come within the scope of the Department of Health, Education and Welfare, although, before it took action, funds were being spent on assisting the poor with family planning by the Office of Economic Opportunity (established in 1964 as part of the Great Society program). On January 24, 1966 HEW appeared to move when Secretary John Gardner issued a statement that the Department would

> conduct and support programs of basic and applied research on population dynamics, fertility, sterility and family planning . . . would conduct and support training programs, collect and make available relevant data, support on request health programs making family planning information and services available and provide family planning information and services on request to individuals who receive health services from operating agencies of the Department.[171]

In fact, HEW subsequently moved very slowly, although in July 1967 family planning was designated as one of six special priority areas; Assistant Secretary Philip Lee was given responsibility for the area and the following month Katherine Oettinger was appointed Deputy Assistant Secretary for Population and Family Planning.

In the Ford Foundation, David Bell, who had been successively Director of the Bureau of the Budget and AID, suggested to Harkavy that Foundation officers should understand more about government and policy and to this end Harkavy was supported by the Foundation in Washington for the summer. Almost immediately he was invited by Lee to prepare a report on the implementation of HEW policy on family planning and population, and this he did between August and September in collaboration with Frederick Jaffe of Planned Parenthood-World Population and Samuel Wishik from Columbia University's International Institute for the Study of Human Reproduction.

The Report recommended the drawing up of a national plan for reaching five million women needing publicly assisted family planning services, the training and assigning of professional staff in the field, the development of HEW staff and the use of Federal funds to assist the States. A recommendation of immediate importance to the phasing out of the Ford Foundation's programs was that 'Immediate steps should be taken to offer training at population studies centers and other appropriate facilities to professionals assigned to family planning staff positions.' This was followed by another recommendation that the National Institutes of Health 'should continue and expand support of non-biomedical research and training in population problems at university population studies centers. . . .' Another recommendation was the

> development of a greatly expanded program of research in fundamental and applied reproductive biology. . . . It is estimated that an 'optimum' world-wide research program would require $150 million a year—about a five-fold increase over present expenditures in the area by Government, foundations and pharmaceutical firms.[172]

This estimate had been made several months earlier in an internal memorandum of the Foundation by Southam and Harkavy. The estimate stated the advisability that $65 million of this money should be channeled through universities. It might be noted that world expenditure on such research, as measured in constant 1965 dollars, actually peaked in 1972–3 at $91 million, three times the 1967 level (when 74 percent of expenditure was of American origin, split up as follows: Government, 45 percent; foundations, 16 percent; industry, 13 percent).[173]

An internal report was not likely to have much impact on Congress. However, as early as April 1965 Senator Ernest Gruening of Alaska had introduced a bill recommending the appointment of Assistant Secretaries for population problems in both the Department of State and HEW. Although the bill was never enacted, influential and widely publicized hearings were held upon it over the next two years and the HEW report was presented as evidence.

In 1968 President Johnson directed the National Institute for Child Health and Human Development (NICHD) to set up a Center for Population Research which was finally established, from the beginning of 1970, with Philip Corfman as Director and Arthur Campbell as Deputy Director, with the mandate that it was 'responsible for the primary Federal effort in population research.' NICHD itself dated back to 1966 and had already provided funds to Michigan's Population Studies Center for its work in Taiwan. From the first year of its establishment, 1970, the NICHD Center for Population Research began to fund university Population Centers and to provide fellowships for American students. In these Centers Ford Foundation and Population Council fellowship money began increasingly to be used for foreign students, especially those from the Third World, but the shadow of future difficulties in supporting such students in American programs had already begun to fall across the scene.

Because of the time-lag in government budgeting, all recommendations in the 1967 Report had been for the Financial Year 1969. In the outcome, HEW Public Health Service Funds for Family Planning rose gradually from $4.6 million in 1965 to $9.7 million in 1968, and then jumped to $14.7 million in 1969 because of the provision in the Child Health Act of 1967 that not less than 6 percent of annual expenditure should be on family planning.

The strongest feelings had been aroused by the possibility of American technical aid in the population field. In 1962 Leona Baumgartner, who had been with Notestein on the

1955 mission to India, joined AID from her previous post as Commissioner of the New York City Health Department and pressed for population activities. In 1963 Congress amended the Foreign Assistance Act to provide funds to support research on problems of population growth. Bell, then head of AID, saw President Kennedy for a definition of how far AID could go and was given an informal but broad hint by Kennedy saying he might use as a guideline the 'practice' of American Catholics. In January, 1965 the AID Office of Population was created and the following year Reimart Ravenholt was appointed Director, a post he was to hold for fifteen decisive years. In fact, there had been a population unit in AID as early as June, 1964 and it made recommendations on population policy in December, 1964 almost certainly influencing the State of the Union Message the following month. In March 1965 AID missions abroad were informed that the Agency was moving into the population field and that technical asssistance could be offered with regard to family planning.

Nevertheless, funds provided by Congress for foreign aid in this area remained around $10.5 million per annum from 1965 through to 1967. This situation was examined in the Population Crisis Hearings of the Senate Subcommittee on Foreign Aid Expenditures in late 1967. In May of that year AID had already announced that it could now help with the supply of contraceptives but by this time shortage of funds had become the major restriction. General William Draper gave evidence to these hearings, employing material that he and Phyllis Piotrow had prepared. However, Draper had decided that such hearings did not have the desired impact on members of the Congress unless their attention was specifically drawn to the argument and he began a major lobbying operation during which he spoke to most members of both the House of Representatives and the Senate. This activity, plus information that Ravenholt was now supplying, were probably the main reasons that funds for the AID population program increased from $10.5 million in 1967 to $34.6 million in 1968 and $45.4 million in 1969, reaching $123 million by 1972. AID money was increasingly available to American University Population programs for overseas activities and led to the dramatic growth of some programs such as that at the University of North Carolina. AID objectives were usually different from those of university research programs and almost every major figure in these programs expressed worry to us about their relations with AID, using such phrases as 'very directive' and 'not conducive to real research.' Much strain developed about the nature of evaluation. Indeed, it was a clash between the AID Population Branch and the International Division of the US Bureau of Census on the extent of fertility decline in Third World countries which led in 1976 to Congress funding the National Academy of Science to undertake a major study of demographic trends.[174]

Meanwhile, the situation on the international scene was also changing. During the first half of 1965 both the United Nations and the World Bank sent missions to India to advise on its family planning program. In May the World Health Organization authorized the development of an advisory program, while in June the Government Council of UNICEF and the Economic and Social Council recommended activities in the population field. On December 10, 1966 the Secretary General of the United Nations issued a Statement by Twelve Heads of State calling for action in the population area.[175] Much of the inspiration and drafting came from Berelson at the Population Council. In December 1966 the United Nations General Assembly called on all United Nations Agencies to draw up plans for assistance in the population field in training, research, information, and advisory services. By May, 1967, an ECOSOC Committee was recommending a stronger action component in United Nations assistance and between June and October, 1967 UNICEF, ILO, and UNESCO all decided to enter the field. In August, 1967 U Thant proposed an action program and fund that led to the establishment of the United Nations Trust Fund for Population

Activities, which changed its name in 1969 to UNFPA when it really became operational. By 1973 the UNFPA budget was $52 million, of which the United States provided almost 40 percent. UNFPA became a fund of the UN General Assembly in 1972 and a subsidiary organ of the UN General Assembly in 1979 with the UNDP Governing Council designated as its governing body. In 1968, following the assumption of its presidency by Robert McNamara, the World Bank also became involved in population activities.

The International Planned Parenthood Federation also loomed large on the international scene from 1965 when first the Victor Fund, organized by General Draper and then SIDA, the Swedish International Development Agency, began to provide it with substantial funds (SIDA had been funding population activities since 1958, the first government agency of a developed country to do so). By 1972 IPPF had a budget of $17 million which grew to $30 million in 1973 and to $42 million in 1974, with AID providing about one-third.

In 1966 national family planning programs were announced by Egypt, Morocco, Malaysia, Kenya, Chile, Tunisia, Singapore, Jamaica, and Barbados, and these were followed in 1967 by Iran, Colombia, Sri Lanka, Costa Rica, and Trinidad and Tobago. There appeared to be little impact on the international stage from the rejection in November 1966 by the Pope of the report by the Papal Commission on oral contraception and by the issuing in July 1968 of *Humanae Vitae* confirming the Roman Catholic Church's traditional stand on contraception. Indeed, in 1967, France passed a new liberal law on contraception which also influenced francophone countries in Africa.

In the United States a long battle of the family planning movement was finally won on July 7, 1965, when the Supreme Court struck down Connecticut's birth control law as unconstitutional.

Third World university programs

By the mid-1960s a situation was developing where the training capacity in universities in America (as well as in France, Britain, Australia, and Canada) were capable of meeting much of the need for training in the developed world and where it appeared there would probably be increasing governmental support for such programs. This was not the position in the Third World with regard to university education, for the United Nations Demographic Training Centres had not developed the relations with universities that had been anticipated a decade earlier. Some Third World university population programs were beginning to develop, such as that at the University of Ghana from 1960 with Population Council assistance. Notestein had long held that only indigenous programs would lead governments to national population policies and to fertility control programs. From 1964 such university programs were supported by the Ford Foundation as the occasion arose but there was no rush to get several moving at once. The first was in the Philippines and it proved to be the clearest example of the Notestein dictum. It was the most highly educated country in Third World Asia and it had the lowest death rate, but, since it was the continent's only predominantly Catholic country, the issue of contraception was not merely a question of demand but of ideology and politics as well.

The Southeast Asian mission of Hauser, Harkavy, and Kirk of late 1962 investigated the possibility of establishing population programs in Southeast Asia. They recommended that such programs should have the backing of universities in developed countries, particularly in the United States, and discussed the possibility that such programs should be built around trained demographers who were returning to their own countries. At the time the only possibility of this kind was Mercedes Concepcion who was completing her doctoral program at the University of Chicago. Accordingly, in November, 1962, the mission discussed with the University of the Philippines the possibility of establishing a Population Center at the University and suggested the likelihood of the return of Concepcion and of the willingness to provide backing by the University of Chicago's Population Research and Training Center. For almost two years this possibility was worked upon by the University of the Philippines, the Ford Foundation Regional Office and the Foundation in New York. It was spurred by the First Asian Population Conference organized in December 1963 in Delhi by the United Nations Economic Commission for Asia and the Far East (later ESCAP), where the need for Asian teaching programs was vigorously discussed. The grant was finally approved on September 11, 1964, two months before the University of the Philippines officially established the Population Institute.

The application for funding took the form of a joint approach from the Universities of the Philippines and Chicago, incorporating an agreement of cooperation between Concepcion and Hauser. In successive grants covering the next decade the Foundation contributed over $700,000, of which the majority went to the University of Chicago for support services including the provision of expatriate Research Associates. There were seven of these, including Frank Lorimer, Peter Smith, Thomas Pullum, and John Laing, and in addition Hauser visited regularly. The link with Chicago lasted until the end of 1974.

The aims of the funding have been analyzed as:

(1) to support the development of the Institute's MA program and other teaching activities;
(2) to promote staff development;
(3) to provide financial and technical assistance in developing a research program; and

(4) to assist in the public information activities of the Institute.

The first proposal from the University of the Philippines spoke of rapid population growth and grossly defective vital statistics:

> In order to obtain an adequate basis for the analysis of the present trends in population and population projections and a continuing flow of demographic intelligence for use by the government in planning economic and social programs, there is great need for a nucleus of competent demographic personnel and provision for their effective utilization.

The plans were to admit fifteen students per year, to produce analyses of population characteristics and trends, and to initiate research programs, with the University of Chicago providing assistance and consultation. The Ford Foundation emphasized

> the importance of the population problem and the desirability of bringing all work together under one program and giving population studies the coherence and drive which does not appear to be possible without a well-defined demographic program. This may well lead in time to a strengthening of the presently weak national interest in the question of population control.

The Population Institute was established in the downtown University of the Philippines campus, a fact frequently deplored by the Foundation. After twenty years, in 1984, a decision was announced for a Department of Demography at the main Diliman campus in Quezon which would incorporate the program, but this was subsequently postponed. The separation meant that the Population Institute was isolated from the other social sciences and, although it had a good demographic library, from the broader social science library facilities. The program used its fellowships to attract about ten students a year and produced in the first decade fifteen MAs, much in accordance with the wider University of the Philippines pattern of enrollment and withdrawal. As planned, several persons, mostly faculty members, went to Chicago for the doctorate although a decade later Professor Concepcion was still the only Filipino with a doctorate in the Institute.

The interrelation between research and the provision of public information was brilliant and led directly to the adoption of a national population policy six years after the establishment of the Institute. In 1965 the Institute released population projections for the Philippines, based largely on the work of the first Research Associate, Frank Lorimer, provided by the Population Council. These projections indicated for 1960 a crude birth rate of 45 per thousand, a crude death rate of 13 per thousand, and a resulting rate of population growth of 3.2 percent per annum. A paper on the projections was the central document for the nation's first population conference in 1965, at which politicians and public servants expressed astonishment at the size of the population projected for the year 2000. There were still substantial doubts as to whether any demand for fertility control was likely to develop among Filipinos but these were answered by a series of KAP surveys between 1965 and 1968 which indicated that women of reproductive age in the present situation would ultimately average seven live births, although most would have preferred fewer, while the majority of women over thirty years of age would prefer to have no more children. The Institute produced a series of publications such as *Philippine Population: Profiles, Prospects and Problems*, 'When Will the Hundred Millionth Filipino be Born?'; 'The Population Problem in the Philippines', and 'What is Happening to the Philippine Birth Rate?' The Institute conducted a series of workshops for the Philippines Press Institute and provided a stream of informed demographic material for the press, radio, and television. Seminars were held in academic and governmental institutions throughout the country. There can be no doubt that these activities hastened the announcement of a national population policy in 1970 and of the Population Act of August 15, 1971 which established the Population Commission and a national family planning program. The legislation specified that the head of the Population Institute would be an ex-officio member of the Population Commission. Thereafter, the Population Commission, which had no research capacity of its own, commissioned the Population Institute to undertake most of its research.

Mercedes Concepcion also played a major role as Chairman of the Organization of Demographic Associates, and in addition filled other important posts in Asia and beyond, such as the presidency of the IUSSP. National Demographic Surveys were carried out in collaboration with the Census Bureau in 1968 and 1972 but not subsequently because of the taking of the World Fertility Survey in 1978. AID funded a Family Planning Evaluation Office attached to the Population Institute. In recent years the Population Institute has also carried out research as part of the ASEAN Project funded first by the World Bank and then by the Australian Development Assistance Bureau. The original plans for the Institute were least successful in terms of staff development due either to the failure of those with doctorates to return or to their obtaining other positions in the Philippines or abroad shortly after their return.

The next funding approach from a Third World program came in 1966 from Egypt although a grant was not made until 1968. The Foundation had worked for fifteen years prior to 1968 with the American University of Cairo, an English-medium university incorporated in Washington DC. It is small and concentrates on the humanities and social sciences. Only very recently have its degrees been recognized for employment in Egypt. There has been a selective process regarding who chooses to become students and faculty and Americans have been welcome there even at times when Egypt has been politically suspicious of the United States.

It has been easy to work with both for this reason and because its whole academic structure has been of an American type and this is particularly the case with regard to the social sciences. There have also been losses. Faculty members have often been more influential and better known in the outside world than in Egypt. The University of Cairo would have been much more difficult to work with but would have been more influential.

Even before the Second World War, both the outside world and Egyptians themselves were conscious of Egypt's population densities and their possible implications. Professor Mohamed Awad, much later the Director General of ILO, had been a delegate to the 1929 International Population Union Conference in Rome and had returned to Egypt to write a book in Arabic, *The Population of this Planet*. He was a founder (Soliman Huzayyin was another) in 1936 of the organization called ROWAD, or Pioneers of Thought, which regularly discussed population matters. Meanwhile, W. Wendell Cleland was at the American University in Cairo writing his book.

In 1953 the Social Sciences Research Center was established with Ford Foundation funding at the American University of Cairo with the enthusiastic cooperation of Cleland who was temporarily back as President. In the same year the National Population Commission was established. During the 1950s the Government was not sympathetic to family planning. Nevertheless, an Egyptian Population Association was formed with a membership containing some very influential persons: Awad, Huzayyin, El Shaffei (who was to be the first head of the Cairo Demographic Centre), and Hanna Rizk (demographer and later Vice President of the American University in Cairo). The Ford Foundation began to fund the study of the migration of Nubians from the area which was to be flooded by the Aswan High Dam through a grant to the AUC Social Science Research Center. President Nasser was shaken by the 1960 Census which counted 26 million people, demonstrating a growth in population since the 1937 Census four millions higher than the Government had believed. Following the break with Syria, the National Charter was issued in 1962. Huzayyin was Secretary of the Preparatory Committee and the Charter contained a statement on problems of population growth. In 1964 Nasser spoke to the Assembly about looming population problems, and in 1965 a Supreme Council for Family Planning was established and the program commenced in 1966.

The United Nations Cairo Demographic Centre had been established in 1963 with El Shaffei as head, later to be succeeded by Huzayyin and then by Mohamed El Badry, and there was a demography component in the statistics program of the University of Cairo under Abdelmegid Farrag. The 1966 Census had recorded more than 30 million population and led to estimates of a crude birth rate of 40, a crude death rate of 17, and a growth rate of 2.3 percent per annum. At the American University of Cairo Leila Hamamsy was Director of the Social Science Research Center and Saad Gadalla was Deputy Director. Lenni Kangas of the Ford Foundation's Regional Office discussed with them the possibility of a substantial population component in the Center's program. The Ford Foundation had already begun to fund two experimental family planning projects through medical schools.

In 1966 the Ford Foundation received a proposal for a Joint Population Research Program to be carried out by the American University in Cairo Social Research Center, the Harvard Center for Population Studies (with which Hammamsy had links), and the Carolina Population Center (with which Gadalla had links). The model was that suggested by the 1963 mission to Southeast Asia and incorporated in the 1964 funding of the University of the Philippines Population Institute. However, the situation changed dramatically with the 1967 war between Egypt and Israel and the departure from the country of most foreigners. A revised funding application, solely from the American University in Cairo, was forwarded as a result and was funded in August of that year. The revised budget was for $236,000, the same as the original but with the almost complete elimination of funds for Visiting Professors and consultants and their replacement by additional funding for fellowships to train faculty in America and for faculty travel costs overseas. The revised project states its aims as:

(a) to undertake scientific research on significant aspects of the population problem in Egypt;
(b) to aid population control efforts . . . by offering scientific information necessary for the National Family Planning Program and for formulating governmental policies and action programs;
(c) to provide training for the junior staff of the Institute and to provide the Institute with additional qualified staff; and
(d) to enable senior staff of the Institute to visit population centers abroad and to attend conferences.

The Ford Foundation recommended the funding to allow 'the Social Research Center to initiate a broad social research and training program in the population area and to provide information for the Government Family Planning Program.'

For the next fifteen years the Social Research Center was to be predominantly involved in population work. It did not institute a teaching program although some faculty members taught in other AUC MA degree programs or supervised students with a population interest. The AUC did not have a doctoral program. What it did most thoroughly was staff development and it successfully sent off five junior staff for doctorates in the United States, of whom all returned to the Center and all but one are still there.

The original research plans were very ambitious but subsequently the research program concentrated on investigating and providing experimental demonstration and change inputs into Gadalla's home town in the Menoufia Governorate. This work was later extended to three centers and produced a well-known book demonstrating the social resistances to fertility decline.[176] With one exception, the Menoufia Project did not deliver contraception but relied on the national program. It experimented with various approaches to professionals and the public to increase the use of the program and also experimented with job creation and occupational training in an attempt to induce social and economic change. Its greatest achievement may have been to induce the Government to try a similar approach after 1977 so that by 1983 Gadalla's program and the Government program were, with AID funds, moving to share the country between them with activities of the kind pioneered in Menoufia.

At the American University in Cairo the President had taken action to reduce the dependence of the Social Research Center on population grants and had appointed two Deputy Directors for urban and rural research respectively. Significantly, he had employed university funds, because, although the other Center staff were tenured both during Ford Foundation funding from 1968 until 1976 and with AID project funding thereafter, they had been fully supported by these external funds. Indeed, one of the reasons that the University had been so receptive to population research was that such funding paid 60 percent of all university overheads.

The last major funding decision of this period was to Hacettepe University in Ankara, Turkey, where discussions commenced later than in Egypt but were sufficiently rapidly concluded to lead to earlier funding, in September 1967.

The new military Government in Turkey had envisaged a population element in its 1961–5 Five-Year Plan but implementation did not take place until near the end of the period. However, an agreement between the Government and the Population Council led in 1963 to a KAP study of Turkey.[177] This was a prime example of how the KAP studies were employed not only as instruments of social science investigation but also as programs demanding collaboration and continuing contact and interest in the population field.

As a result, a Population Council representative arrived in 1964 and in the same year the Ministry of Health established a family planning unit within its structure. On April 10, 1965 the Government passed its Family Planning Law allowing the development of a national family planning program from 1966.

The Ford Foundation Representative in Ankara from 1960 to 1969 was Eugene Northrop, a mathematician and former academic dean at the University of Chicago. Frederic Shorter was a product of the Ford Foundation Foreign Area Studies Program and, although his focus had been on South Asia, this was changed to the Middle East when he joined Princeton University. Northrop had been making grants in the social sciences at a new type of university, the Middle East Technical University (METU) and had in 1966 been discussing a grant for a population institute in a still more recent university, Hacettepe, which already had both Ford and Rockefeller Foundation money. Northrop persuaded Shorter to come to Ankara as Program Advisor and as a Visiting Professor of Economics at METU but he soon met Dr Nusret Fisek, Dean of the School of Graduate Studies at the Hacettepe Science Center, which was funded by the Ford Foundation. Fisek was the son of Kemal Atatürk's Chief of Staff and was the driving force behind the development of population studies in Turkey. Funding for the Hacettepe Institute of Population Studies (HIPS) was requested in April, 1967, on two grounds. The first was to develop a graduate program in population dynamics and to encourage the creation of undergraduate population courses in other institutions. The second was the development of an adult education program throughout the community with a greater emphasis on family planning. The Ford Foundation favored funding the project because of the lack of qualified personnel for the family planning program and the need for plans for the population policy, noting that 'Hacettepe could help remedy both these deficiencies by training administrators and by operating first a small pilot program to develop effective procedures, and then a large demonstration project to see what can be done.' The grant was for $375,000 and was the first segment of funds which by the end of the funding program in 1976 would total $879,000. Most of the money was for foreign visiting staff and for fellowships for Turkish faculty and MA graduates to pursue doctorates overseas. In 1967 Shorter transferred his teaching from METU to HIPS.

In some ways the HIPS program was a very traditional demographic one of high caliber. It demonstrated Shorter's link with Princeton's Office of Population Research and the entire faculty, except for the Director, who was from medicine, were social scientists. It produced solid information, trusted by government planners, on demographic levels and trends. It produced four books on Turkish population, all written in Turkish, although one was also translated into English, and numerous papers. Of the thirty-five students who completed the MA degree, one-third went overseas for doctoral programs and almost all the rest secured governmental positions appropriate to their training. The Foundation adopted a policy of helping those with doctorates returning to Turkey to establish themselves in population studies with small grants under a range of Foundation programs. Some went to Hacettepe but most began to teach population studies in other universities.

The program achieved success in two ways. First, government planners and other public servants kept up a strong demand for further information. Second, it was an acceptable academic program with a strong teaching component which entrenched itself at Hacettepe and, through its students, elsewhere. Indeed, the program survived relatively unscathed the political upheaval of the early 1970s, the attacks on the universities and particularly on the social sciences, and even the related dismissal of Fisek from the Directorship of the Institute in 1972. On the other hand, the investment of effort, time, and money into the 1973 National Demographic Survey was not rewarded by adequate follow-up analysis and the latter had to await the 1978 World Fertility Survey. HIPS affected the National Family Planning Program but the latter may only have had a minor impact on the gradual Turkish fertility decline.[178] By 1982 all Turkish university programs appeared to be endangered by the New University Law.

In Indonesia the group who were to play a major role in the development of demography acquired their first interest in the early 1950s when Widjojo Nitisastro, Kartomo Wirosuhardjo, and Tangoantiang (later Iskandar and henceforth referred to as such) all did dissertations or other work on transmigration. Nathan Keyfitz was in Indonesia working with the Department of Statistics and the National Planning Bureau as early as 1953 under the auspices of the US Bureau of Census and he and Widjojo together wrote an influential book[179] in Indonesian on the country's demography (Widjojo, after the establishment of the military Government in 1965, became a close advisor to President Suharto). In 1963 Hauser, Harkavy, and Kirk visited Indonesia and later in the same year Marshall Balfour and Vincent Whitney of the Population Council returned. Iskandar was given a Population Council Fellowship to do the Princeton OPR Course and, on his return in 1964, founded the Demographic Institute within the Faculty of Economics, University of Indonesia. Although the Indonesian delegation to the First Asian Population Conference in Delhi in 1963, headed by Kartomo, had been told to oppose family planning programs, the new Government after 1965 was sympathetic and a family planning program began to be organized by 1970.

In the same year the Population Council provided Gavin Jones as an advisor to the Demographic Institute of the University of Indonesia. On March 16, 1970 the University of Indonesia applied to the Ford Foundation for $37,000 to train university faculty from twenty-two regional Indonesian universities in demography and research methods in three separate batches, each for a one-semester course, over the next eighteen months. The aim was to enable them to teach

demography and to undertake research into interrelated
matters of population, development, and family planning.
Ultimately, during the decade, the Ford Foundation provided funds totalling around $600,000. During the period
1973–5 the standard course was increased to two semesters
and at this time seventy-four university faculty were trained.
During the whole period to the present date 500 persons have
received such training, of whom 150 have been university
faculty. Now the courses are either two or three months in
duration and are most often taken by public servants,
journalists or members of voluntary organizations from
all parts of Indonesia. The foreign input into teaching in the
early 1970s was made by Gavin Jones but later the Ford
Foundation recruited Peter McDonald from the Australian
National University and Jeanne Sinquefield from Bogue's
Center at Chicago. The program produced a demographic
interest, and often a population teaching and research component, in a range of universities across a huge country. Most
of these faculty members need further training and an
increasing number have secured it. Many taught courses with
a population textbook written in Indonesian by McDonald.[180]
The Demographic Institute undertook an increasing research
program including an important Fertility–Mortality Survey
in 1973. The program lost Iskandar when he died in 1977, to
be succeeded by Kartomo. After the Ford Foundation funding came to an end in the late 1970s UNFPA took over.
The major weakness of the Demographic Institute is that it
has never received University permission to erect a Master's
degree program in Population Studies, although current
negotiations with the Faculty of Economics may succeed.
The stumbling block has been the issue of whether population studies should be an area of concentrated study with
a focus on data collection or whether it should be taught
only as part of an older discipline such as economics, with
a greater attention to theory.

   In 1971 Gadjah Mada University established a Population
Studies Center and Masri Singarimbun was attracted back

from the Australian National University's Department of Demography to head it. The Center was provided with a series of advisors from the ANU Department of Demography through the Australian Universities International Development Programme, beginning with Terry and Valerie Hull. In August 1975 the Center held a successful Workshop on Population Research in Indonesia which brought in faculty from regional universities. In 1976 the university proposed to the Ford Foundation that funds should be provided to allow the development of a series of such workshops to enable the faculty of provincial universities to receive further training in the population field in research design, research methods, and analytical techniques. This was funded in 1977 with $165,000 from the Foundation and $65,000 from AID with about half the funds providing consultants and equipment. Many of those attending the workshops had already received some training at the University of Indonesia. The concentration of workshops on specific topics such as family planning, marriage and divorce, and migration and trans-migration (the organized movement of persons from Java to the outer islands) led to continued research links and small-scale funding and to planned cooperative books. From 1981 Gadjah Mada University began to develop the first MA degree (known as an S2 program) in Population in Indonesia.

The later programs

In one sense the establishment of the International Institute for the Study of Human Reproduction at Columbia University was not a later effort of the Ford Foundation. In early 1964, soon after the formation of the Foundation's Population Program, a continuing effort got under way to found a major institution for research and training in human reproduction. Talks continued for over eighteen months and Professor Howard Taylor of the Columbia University Faculty of Medicine became an ever more important participant. When the first formal steps were taken, the Foundation's hopes were clear:

An Institute of Human Reproduction would add a significant dimension to research and training now going forward at medical schools and other institutions. An institute having as its major goal the development of better means of birth control, which can attract fundamental scientists and provide an ideal atmosphere for basic research and training in human reproduction, and can follow up the fundamental work and engage in the development and clinical trial of new contraceptives may yield results faster than if the process were left exclusively in the hands of scattered researchers in institutions directed primarily towards other goals. The establishment of an institute in its own building with an international staff would constitute a public statement of this nation's serious concern with the problem of world over-population and its determination to mobilize scientific resources to meet this challenge. It would serve as an international clearinghouse of research information and as a stimulus of further information efforts around the world. An institute could be a focal point of attraction for high governmental officials and would legitimize and reinforce similar efforts in their own countries.

On October 26, 1965 the Foundation approved an appropration of $8.5 million intended to cover a nine month period, for the initial development of the Institute. In fact, because of a slow start, the appropration was extended by three years and even by 1977 $1.8 million remained unspent and was returned to the Foundation. Long delays occurred in attempting to plan and construct a separate building on a site of its own for the Institute and it was not until 1971 that it was finally agreed this was impossible (because, first, President Nixon cancelled a matching grant for building from the NIH and, later, AID funds for building were not forthcoming) and the Ford Foundation agreed that its money could be used to rent and reconstruct more limited space in a Columbia Faculty of Medicine building.

The original plans for the Institute envisaged several major units, of which three would be biomedical, one would be for clinical family planning, and the other would be devoted to psychology, biometrics and sociology. After, a reorganization in 1975, two separate Centers were created. One was close to the original concept, although less grandoise. This was the Center for Reproductive Sciences which has since carried out distinguished biological and medical research. The other center, the Center for Population and Family Health, was close to the model which had been developed over the previous decade in schools of public health. Soon afterwards another unit, the Center of International Family Planning Programs, was established with additional support from the Ford Foundation. This center was first headed by Samuel Wishik, and, on his retirement, by Allan Rosenfield who moved in 1976 toward institutionlization by persuading Columbia's School of Public Health to incorporate into the divisional structure a Division of Population and Family Health. This was possible because the School had neither a Division of Maternal and Child Health nor one of population and it was agreeable because it did not cost the University very much. Rosenfield is still the only member of the Center on tenure or supported by university funds. As all centers and institutes at Columbia University, the Center has successfully sought private and public funding, including a very innovative program in the Third World providing technical assistance for the establishment of experimental family planning programs. Their students study toward master's degrees and doctorates in public health and usually do not originate in medicine. Ford funding ceased in 1977 but project work in New York City and in the Third World has brought NIH, DHHS (Department of Health and Human Services—previously HEW), AID and foundation funding so that the Department secures considerably greater funding than does the Center for Reproductive Sciences.

When Harkavy began the Foundation's work in 1959 he sought out Ansley Coale for advice and frequent subsequent consultations occurred. Yet Princeton University's Office of Population Research was never a major recipient of Foundation funds. One reason was OPR's early start and the financial arrangements it had already made. Notestein had begun providung a single year-long course in 1936 and this situation did not change for a third of a century until, in the late 1960s, OPR faculty began providing additional courses, mostly through Departments of the University. From the beginning the course was accepted by the Department of Economics as a component of a graduate program and this was true also in the Sociology Department when it was later established. It trained around half of all students on Population Council Demography Fellowships in the 1950s and devised a Certificate to show that the course had been completed. At its height it had thirty-five students and was taken as a Certificate Course by most Third World students and as a post-doctoral program for most Americans. OPR focussed on research and had no MA students, although it shared about three new doctoral students a year with other Departments in which they were enrolled for degree purposes. OPR had been well financed by the Milbank Memorial Foundation, and then by the Rockefeller Foundation and the National Institute of Health. Notestein was apprehensive of large funding from a single source. However, as early as December 1964, OPR applied to the Foundation for a supplementary core grant of $250,000 to extend over ten years. This helped with research and training (especially of Third World students), provided some fellowships and assisted the publication program, in particular reducing the financial difficulties involved in producing *Population Index*, the major bibliographical journal in the demographic field. At the end of the grant, OPR pointed to the names of thirty demographers who were by that time well-known who had been partly supported by it. OPR's major request to the Foundation came in 1969 with a request for $460,000, reduced after discussion to $271,000, to support teaching and research in economic demography. This was the field that brought Coale to Third World interests in the mid-1950s when the World Bank funded him and Edgar Hoover to study India.[181] Nevertheless, it remained an area of neglect and guilt for most population programs. Even OPR had to apologize because they could not spent any of the grant for two and a half years while they looked for a suitable person, finally finding Bryan Boulier. In the meantime the Foundation had also provided $74,000 to OPR in the same area to support Shorter under an arrangement which allowed him to spend most of his time in the Middle East as a consultant for Ford Foundation offices in Ankara, Beirut, and Cairo.

An interesting example of a program which received only late funding was that in the Department of Sociology of Brown University. One reason that it failed to secure earlier funding was the small size of the population program, even in 1960. The Sociology Department had been founded by Vincent Whitney in 1949 and he was succeeded as Chairman by Kurt Mayer and then Sidney Goldstein. The first and the third were from the University of North Carolina and the University of Pennsylvannia respectively and the program initially stressed migration, having only four faculty members even in the late 1950s. The second reason was the lack of interest in the program at this time in either fertility or Third World studies.

The program began to grow in the early 1960s when NIH funded an ageing project and some of the funds were used to bring in Robert Burnight who was known to have fund-raising ability and to encourage him to look for ways to expand the program. He did this initially by developing a program of computer utilization in demographic research and securing an NIH training grant. Almost independently, the Ford Foundation began to support Robert Potter in 1963 to analyze the fertility and family planning data of the Khanna study and to develop new techniques for analysis of this kind. Indeed, the Foundation cared little which institution Potter worked in, although it rather favored Harvard, and he taught no courses at Brown until after 1970. Nevertheless, his work, which had received $400,000 support from the Foundation by 1977, was influential in the Brown Sociology Department. In 1965 a Population Center was founded and the following year a grant was obtained to establish a research program which largely centered on Rhode Island. However, in 1968, Goldstein took study leave to occupy the consultant's post supported by the Population Council in the Population Institute of Chulalongkorn University in Bangkok, Thailand. He was followed to Thailand by Burnight. Goldstein was involved with the Longitudinal Study of Social, Economic and Demographic Change in Thailand.[182]

The program at Brown expanded with NICHD support and developed a reputation for its teaching and pastoral care of students. In 1971 when NICHD support for Brown and other population programs appeared to have been eliminated, an urgent appeal was made to the Ford Foundation for $250,000 to allow the Population Studies and Training Center to operate for another three years. This was granted from February 1972, and, when it was discovered that NICHD would be again forthcoming, the Ford Foundation permitted its grant to stand but extended the period until 1977. By that year the program had twenty-nine graduate students, of whom seven were foreign. That year ten MAs and two doctorates were awarded, and ten graduates secured positions, one of which was in the Third World (in Thailand).

This report will not attempt a detailed examination of the considerable funds that went to Latin America during the 1970s. Since 1955 the Foundation had made a major effort to assist in the establishment of the social sciences in Latin America and had helped found both CEBRAP in São Paulo, Brazil and CEPLAM in Santiago, Chile.

There had been an early interest in demography in the statistical service of Brazil, especially the work of Giorgio Mortara.[183] Stycos and others working with the Population Council had helped with the development of population interests since the 1950s. The major impulse after 1957 was from the UN Demographic Centre in Santiago, CELADE, which, more than any other UN Center, attempted institutional development throughout its region. It avoided political trouble because of the extent to which its training was in formal demography with a lesser social component.

A greater Ford Foundation involvement in population issues was planned by a mission in the early 1970s headed by Coale. One result was that the Foundation supported projects in Brazil which amounted to $1 million by 1977. These included the development of a Master's degree program in population within the Economics Faculty at Bella Horizonte and the support there of both Thomas Merrick and Paul Singer. Much of the Ford support was for projects such as the major study mounted by Elza Berquo at CEBRAP of fertility change throughout Brazil. Students were supported both within the country and for higher studies outside and funds were provided for the establishment of a Brazilian Population Association. Perkin worked with Brazilian professors of obstetrics establishing family planning programs for high-risk mothers in accordance with a check list which he had developed (including socio-economic as well as medical factors) and so helped to establish a basis for the government's acceptance of such work.

Within Spanish-speaking Latin America most support was given in Mexico, Peru, Chile, and Venezuela. This included assistance for establishing teaching programs in the Colegio de Mexico and in the University of Lima. The American university most closely linked was the University of Texas at Austin, which, partly for geographical reasons, had long had Mexican interests. A Sociology Department was founded in 1958 by Leonard Broom who had strong quantitative sociological interests. Harley Browning collaborated with the Argentinians Jorge Balan and Elizabeth Jelin with Foundation support in 1964 on the Monterrey study of Mexican migration.[184] The subsequent establishment of a Population Center at Austin provided a home for Mexican and other Latin American studies.

In April 1976 the Foundation funded the Australian National University for $100,000 over four years to supplement the Department of Demography's special Masters (Demography) Program support, received chiefly, apart from the University, from the Australian Development Assistance Bureau. This program focussed entirely on Third World demography, taking in ten students a year for a two-year course from 1976 and fifteen from the early 1980s.

Increasingly during the 1970s, the Ford Foundation, either on its own or more usually in collaboration with the Rockefeller Foundation or the Population Council, attempted to support Third World population graduates or others who might undertake research and institutionalize population programs through competitions which provided the winners with research grants. This was an extension of the approach first used in Turkey where various Ford funds were used to allow graduates who had secured positions in universities anywhere in the country to continue to do some research work. The plans for a world-wide competition, known as the Population Policy Research Program, were worked out jointly between the Rockefeller and Ford Foundations in

1970 and the first awards were made in 1971.[185] Harkavy had developed the idea and had convinced Lee De Vinney of the Rockefeller Foundation. The competition was generally restricted to a ceiling of around $25,000 in the early years but was subsequently raised to $35,000 and then $50,000. Its aims were listed as the achievement of high-quality population research, the securing of an increase in Third World participation, and the attraction of more social scientists into the area. In 1976, in keeping with post-Bucharest Conference thinking, the title was changed to the Population and Development Policy Research Program. There is no doubt that the competitions largely succeeded in their main aim of consolidating and widening the population network. Yet a report in 1977 had several criticisms.[186] There were relatively few applications from developing countries compared with developed countries and many of them were of lower standard. Many Third World applicants were increasingly dissuaded from entry because of a justifiable anxiety of losing. Their problems were compounded by the requirement that applications must be prepared in English, and Ford Foundation representatives were often unsure of the role that they should play. Some of these problems were subsequently overcome by the development of regional competitions, judged by local panels in the regional area and offering on average smaller grants. In the general population field the MEAWARDs were established for the Middle East, the SEAPRAP competition for Southeast Asia, and PISPAL for Latin America. Between 1974 and 1980 there was also a Latin American competitive research program in human reproduction, PLAMIRH.

The Foundation also increasingly funded other international co-operative efforts. In 1972 it gave $250,000 to the Population Council to help establish ICARP, the International Committee on Applied Research in Population. This organization enrolled as members and contacts a wide range of consultants in established family planning programs. It arranged for meetings of a smaller group of consultants, and it sought research proposals and funded those that were approved. One aim was to improve professionalism in the running of national family planning programs. There was a good deal of introspection about ICARP and it was perhaps not as successful as some of its advocates had hoped.

By the end of the decade the Foundation had also begun to fund Population Dynamics Workshops which were highly specialized and which were evaluated as being very successful both by participants and reviewers. Multivariate Data Analysis Workshops were held in the Asian Institute of Technology, Bangkok in 1970 and 1980 and at the Bogazici University, Istanbul. In the latter year a more substantive meeting was held in Lima, Peru, with funding from both the Ford and Rockefeller Foundations, on the Dynamics of Fertility in the Andean Region.

The Ford Foundation changes course

Some of the reasons that the Ford Foundation decreased its population funding are inherent in the way foundations work. They have limited funds compared with governments and hence seek to do what is innovational and to enter areas where small investments can have a marked impact.

The events of 1967 and 1968 which led to a great increase in HEW money for population activities within the United States and in AID funding for external activities led some to wonder whether the Foundation had already played its role. This was reinforced on the world scene as UNFPA and IPPF began to gather strength. In addition, during the second half of the 1960s, as country after country announced a population policy, and as it became clearer that birth rates were falling in parts of East and Southeast Asia and that some change might be beginning in Latin America as had already happened in parts of the Caribbean, then it began to be suggested that Foundation funds might be used to catalyze change in other fields. However, the changes occurring were more complex than this simple version of success in meeting an original aim.

Firstly, there was a crisis of confidence about the worth-whileness and moral case for technical aid. The consensus of the 1950s was broken. The debates of the late 1960s over Vietnam led to many of both liberal and conservative persuasions concluding, for very different reasons, that overseas involvement on a large scale was undesirable. This was reinforced by apparent failure in some development areas, even though economists pointed out that per capita income in the Third World had grown during the 1960s, in spite of earlier fears that it would not, and indeed that it had increased more rapidly than had been the case in Europe or North America during the Industrial Revolution. Enthusiasm for development aid also waned as Third World countries were increasingly attracted by political developmental theories distinguishing between the center and the periphery which argued both that technical aid could not lead to development and that it was never meant to.[187] Within the population field there was an increasing loss of confidence as to whether family planning programs implied a single-theme Malthusian approach to development. This argument was employed not only in the Third World but also in continental Europe where it led both to the formation of an Anti-Malthusian Forum parallel to the Tribune at the 1974 Bucharest World Population Conference and to a crisis of confidence in the Swedish International Development Authority, encouraging its retreat from the population field. Confidence was also undermined by suggestions from other quarters that family planning programs were feeble instruments when vast social changes were required. At the end of 1967 Kingsley Davis had published 'Population Policy: Will Current Programs succeed? Grounds for skepticism concerning the demographic effectiveness of family planning are considered.'[188] Davis charged that the programs were concerned only with families and that their goals were far too weak. He said that much of the success in increasing contraception was as a substitute for illegal abortion which would have been effective in any case. 'Popular enthusiasm for family planning is found mainly in the cities, or in advanced countries such as Japan and Taiwan where people would adopt contraception in any case, program or no program.' The growing strength of the Women's Movement also added complexities. The movement had very considerable potential for supporting the family planning movement in that it regarded fertility control as every woman's right and as an essential key to women controlling their own destinies, but they regarded these matters as perhaps more important than economic development and were wary of programs that did not include the issue of women.

Some of the problems of the population movement arose from reactions to exaggerated or emotional claims from their own supporters. Such reactions were clearly provoked by the publication in 1968 of Paul Ehrlich's book, *The Population Bomb*,[189] which in its paperback form had a subtitle on the cover, 'Population Control or Race to Oblivion?' It also noted on the title page that both the phrases 'population bomb' and 'population explosion' had been employed as early as 1954 in a pamphlet issued by the Hugh Moore Fund. The first chapter described Ehrlich's emotional conversion on finding himself in a Delhi slum one night and observing a situation which has been repeatedly pointed out in the Third World to be poverty rather than the product of rapid population growth. The publication four years later of the report by the Club of Rome also in the long run probably had a net negative impact on those who wished to attempt to arrive at the most accurate possible assessments of the role of population growth and of achieved population size in economic development.[190]

Much of the debate focussed on the United Nations World Population Conference held in Bucharest in August 1974. The Conference produced almost unanimous agreement on an amended Plan of Action but in many ways it proved a turning point. The maxim, 'Development is the best contraceptive' was widely expressed and it became clear that many developing countries were apprehensive of the fertility control ingredient in development being over-stressed. Many of the delegates were startled when the clearest case against the reliance on fertility-control intervention as a single cure-all was put by John D. Rockefeller 3rd.[191] The meeting was probably nothing more than a salutary reminder that the problem was as complex as had been clearly seen twenty years earlier but had been forgotten in the rhetoric and euphoria of the late 1960s. However, Mauldin, Choucri, Notestein, and Teitelbaum clearly believed that harm had been done in the reluctance of the Conference to single out population as the important variable and in its deletion of population targets, even though they did stress the agreement in the Plan on the necessity for making available contraceptive advice and services to all persons.[192]

The industrialized world too was entering a more conservative era, which had implications for contraceptive programs even though contraception for married couples was decreasingly attacked. The atmosphere had not changed when in January 1970 the US Post Office issued a family planning stamp, an action which gave rise to some criticism, or at the end of the year when President Nixon signed the *Family Planning and Population Research Act*. This legislation created the Federal Office of Population Affairs and confirmed that federal money could be used for family planning services for poor Americans. An amendment to the Act had implications for future controversies in that it barred the use of any funds when abortion was involved. This occurred just at a time when most Asian family planning programs, which had considerable American support, were envisaging abortion as a more important future element in their armory. The battle lines of the future began to appear shortly after the US Supreme Court, in January 1973, forbade the interference with a woman's right to have an abortion during the first three months of pregnancy. The official enquiry into America's population began at a time when it was widely felt that the country would benefit from a decline in the rate of natural increase, but issued its report[193] in 1972 at a time when the need was rather for urging sanguinity about the low levels already attained.

As early as 1970 the struggle had begun in New York State and California over the right to provide minors with contraception without the permission of their parents or without the parents being informed. This led by 1980 to a Federal Appeals Court ruling that parents need not be told, and an attempt by the Government in 1982 to reverse this ruling. By the mid-1970s the Right to Life Movement had placed on the public agenda such questions as the right to abortion, the funding of abortion for the poor by Medicaid, and the provision of contraception to minors. It was inevitable that the internal debate on aspects of fertility control would influence views on fertility control elsewhere in the world and the consensus on the use of government funds for fertility control.

Part of the explanation for the erosion of previous support probably lay in demographic trends in the West. The slow decline in birth rates in the 1960s had been followed by a more rapid and unpredicted fall in the 1970s so that in North America, most of Europe, Japan, and Australasia birth rates were below long-term replacement levels, indeed as low as those reached transiently only once before and that in the economic crisis of the 1930s. In some countries of Europe the annual numbers of deaths already exceeded the number of births. In the United States governmental assistance for family planning had long exhibited an Achilles' heel, which was always likely to prove controversial. Government support had begun in the South, in North Carolina, even before the Second World War, and the majority of the poor recipients of publicly supported family planning services were black. Even in the 1960s there had been talk of black genocide, and the internal American debate has had a considerable impact on African political attitudes. That debate was particularly lively in the early 1970s when Dick Gregory wrote in October 1971 in *Ebony* that the black man's answer to genocide was to have big families and when in April 1972 the National Association of Black Social Workers rejected a proposal to support family planning.

The situation continued to change in the United States after the 1980 elections when the Government passed into the hands of a socially and economically conservative coalition. The social conservatives were not always in an easy coalition with the economic conservatives and were not always sure of their support (as comments by Barry Goldwater have clearly shown). The social conservatives were basically religious and opposed to abortion and often to sexual relations and concomitant contraceptive practice outside marriage. The family planning scene began to change. By 1981 the University of Chicago was not enthusiastic about Bogue applying for a further grant to continue the kind of work he had been doing during the late 1970s. The AID Population Program was unlikely to maintain a high profile once Ravenholt lost the leadership in 1981. The challenge to the Coale and Hoover view, that rapid population growth was necessarily harmful to the rate of economic growth,[194] was made in a widely read book by Julian Simon[195] and in articles and a report by Nick Eberstadt.[196] By late 1982 Government funding was being refused for highly respected journals on international fertility control if they merely reported the employment of abortion.[197] *The New York Times*, which had published an editorial on October 4, 1977 warning that America was slipping backwards on the abortion issue, published a particularly hard-hitting editorial on these new pressures which they regarded as a form of censorship.[198]

However, one can probably date the Ford Foundation's cut-backs in population funding to the stock market collapse of the early 1970s which dramatically affected both the Ford and Rockefeller Foundations' finances. In terms of real dollars the foundations were shrinking and they were looking for programs which were believed to have reached their targets and which could be eliminated. From 1970 every funding of a university population program was described as probably terminal although renewals were reasonably frequent until about 1975. The last appointment was made to the staff of the Foundation's population program in 1977 and most posts were terminated in 1981, the program slowly dwindling thereafter.

The major activity of the final period was ensuring that certain selected university population programs continued. All the chosen programs in the United States had NICHD support but this support came in the form of a series of grants for core support, library, research, etc. and were highly specific. Every program said that its future, particularly its contacts with the Third World and its ability to train Third World students, would be endangered if it possessed no flexible money of the kind that had been represented by previous Foundation grants. They all argued that flexibility made for efficiency and economy. The solution was a system of matching tie-off grants.

The major concern was with the viability of the Population Council and debate and investigations continued for four years. The solution was twofold. In September 1980 the Council was given $2½ million for general purposes support over the years 1981–4. Finally, in January 1981, the Council was given a tie-off grant of $5 million for its John D. Rockefeller 3rd Memorial Fund provided that other donors could be found to raise a further $10 million. The Council did this mostly by going to other foundations and the total $15 million formed the core of the $25 million which they planned to reach in the Memorial Fund, and in fact did reach, by 1983.

The same formula of 2:1 matching grants was employed with the selected university population programs, those at Brown, the Population Studies Center at Michigan, and Princeton's Office of Population Research. The matching funds were obtained by the Brown President from the outside community and by OPR largely from university funds in an exceptionally well-endowed university. Michigan used both sources during a difficult period when the State's economy was in unusually bad shape.

Overseas, the University of the Philippines Population Institute also received a tie-off grant, but, with a recognition of likely difficulties, only parity in matching was required.

What was achieved?

The achievements can be measured in various ways, each of them within the bounds of the aims and interests of the Ford Foundation. Nevertheless, there is little doubt that the larger interest of the Population Program was the controlling of population growth rates. The social science viewpoint up until at least 1950 was that birth rates were unlikely to fall in the Third World until there had been profound social and economic change involving at least massive urbanization and probably even considerable industrialization. This was certainly necessary to create a consumer demand for fertility control but was also probably necessary to ensure that Governments decided to provide family planning programs. After all, Governments in the West had moved much more cautiously and slowly than had their citizens. This was why Notestein was so surprised when the Indian Government began to move in the early 1950s toward a family planning program. By 1960 there was growing confidence that efficient family planning programs might have a major impact even on agrarian populations.

There has been a substantial degree of success of two types. First, most countries in Asia have decided to erect national family planning programs and there are a considerable number of programs in other parts of the world as well. Second, birth rates have fallen widely in the Third World and may well continue to fall. The change in Latin America is much in accord with the earlier theory of fundamental social change needed for demographic transition and agrees on the whole with *threshold theory* which sets out the social and economic levels to be attained before fertility decline begins.[199] This was also generally true in the case of East and mainland Southeast Asia. The proportions of population in agriculture were often higher than they had been in the Western transition but so were the levels of education and increasingly the role of education was debated.[200] Two features stood out. The first was that birth rates had often declined faster than had been the case in the West, particularly in Japan. The second was the evidence that government-led fertility declines were taking place in three huge countries containing between them two-fifths of the population of the world and well over half the population of the developing world, China, India, and Indonesia. The central questions relate to how this happened, what role the West played and how the Ford Foundation fitted into the whole picture.

These are the kind of questions that the authors of this book have been attempting to answer in Third World work over the last quarter of a century. It has been the focus of our work while living or working in Southeast Asia, South Asia, sub-Saharan Africa, and the Middle East.[201] It was the area of a specific investigation during 1968-9, supported by the Population Council and concentrating on Korea, Taiwan, Philippines, Hong Kong, Indonesia, Singapore, Pakistan (including East Pakistan, now Bangladesh), Iran, and Turkey.[202] That investigation involved identifying large numbers of people who had played roles in policy formulation and implementation during the move to the adoption of population policies, employing both oral and documentary evidence. The area was so complex that the investigation has never been completed or adequately reported. Nevertheless, the direction indicated by the findings was so fascinating that it was a powerful inducement to undertake the investigation necessary for this report because it appeared to us that more of the explanation of the changes occurring lay in the kind of matters analyzed here than we had first anticipated.

It did appear that a minimum of technological change in birth control had been necessary. Except where abortion was readily accepted by the population, as in Japan, or sterilization accepted by the government, as in India, massive change had awaited the era of IUDs and oral contraception. The evidence seemed to be that societies could not move quickly to the use of withdrawal as a contraceptive method unless some experience and acceptance of it had long been in the culture. This would not necessarily have been true if the fertility declines were to be as slow as they were in France in the nineteenth century or if the societies had awaited the levels of occupational change that occurred at the end of the nineteenth century in north-western Europe or English-speaking countries of overseas European settlement. But the contraceptive innovations were a necessary precursor to most Asian fertility declines of the 1960s and 1970s (though this was not necessarily the case in Singapore and Hong Kong where fertility declines were already underway by 1960, although in a socio-economic context closer to that of earlier Europe or contemporary Latin America).

Nor did what occurred depend on birth control technology developed after the early 1960s. Copper-coated IUDs, lower dosage pills, and suction abortions may have made birth control somewhat more acceptable but they have probably speeded the declines only marginally. The investment of over $100 million by the Ford Foundation and perhaps $1.5 billion from all sources over the last twenty years into biomedical research into human reproduction and family planning may well make life easier by the end of the century but the evidence seems to be fairly clear that there has been little impact so far on making possible that Third World fertility transition which has so far taken place. It is, of course, quite possible that this impact is still to come, and it is quite true that the lack of appeal of existing methods of fertility control is one aspect of the failure of the birth rate in sub-Saharan Africa to decline.

On the other hand, it does appear that social demographers in the 1940s misunderstood Asian society (and they may now misunderstand African and Middle Eastern society because of their recent Asian experience). They did not understand societies which were not like those created by

Christianity, Islam or Judaism, where there was no strict religion of the Book and no continuing tension between state and revealed morality. Nor did they understand societies which had old traditions of abortion or infanticide. It became increasingly clear that social leadership could play a role in fertility control in East Asia, Southeast Asia, and non-Moslem South Asia that was inconceivable in Europe, Latin America or the Middle East, and, for different reasons, in Africa. Indeed, the ultimate problem for the West is how closely it is prepared to associate with family planning programs that are not merely efficient but also coercive. The evidence showed ever more clearly that the existence of a family planning program was of significance, as was its efficiency of operation,[203] although care was not always observed to identify the extent to which consumer demand determined at least part of that efficiency.

The more we followed up leads in the oral histories of these programs, the more it appeared that individuals had played decisive, if often obscure, roles at every level. Regimes which were oriented toward rapid technological change, often military governments or authoritarian civilian ones, were perhaps more likely to turn toward experts for suggestions about how social or demographic change might keep pace with technical progress or augment it. However, democratically elected governments in South and Southeast Asia in ex-British colonies also turned to the civil service for planning advice. We attempted to identify all those who gave advice and to establish the basis for their viewpoint. This was sometimes local experience, but even then it was usually augmented by overseas experience or ideas. More often it was largely the latter alone.

The whole context of changing viewpoint and advice was one of a network of ideas. The wider control was, of course, that of newspapers, magazines, books, radio, and television. The world debate certainly moved some political leaders into a frame of mind where they were prepared to accept demographic initiatives. Yet action was usually taken and continued on the advice of individuals. These individuals had surprisingly frequently taken degrees in the main population programs, or had taken some courses with these programs, or had taken economics degrees where they were lectured by faculty with part-time connections with the population programs.

This finding raises the whole question of how the programs achieved this kind of impact. One of our main purposes in the 1982–3 project for this report was to talk to present and past students in an effort to determine this. It is clear that many of their courses, especially those in schools of public health, stated or implied that great advantage was to be secured, or alternatively disaster was to be averted, by successful organized efforts to reduce birth rates. This does not, however, appear to be anything like the full story. These programs quite clearly developed a 'hidden curriculum.'[204] The interaction between students and faculty and between students themselves, as well as the very fact of the programs, led most students into a stronger feeling than they had possessed on arrival that they were part of a movement to reduce fertility levels. Some also saw it as a new and successful profession but even they almost always experienced ideological conversion also. Over a thousand students secured graduate qualifications in population[205] and the majority did so in programs or institutions where Ford Foundation money had played a significant role in establishing or continuing the program.

A separate question arises with regard to the subject matter that was taught. The answer, rather surprisingly, may be clearer with regard to the more formal demographic programs where Foundation money was often taken to allow academics to pursue interests and to teach programs which they wanted to do for their own sake. The more formal the program the more professional did its product seem to be and the more confident were administrators and politicians in the academic's advice. Indeed, they increasingly accepted the analyses of these local experts rather than looking to foreigners. This was precisely the situation that Notestein had believed to be necessary. The situation is more difficult to judge with regard to courses on family planning administration. Many of the trainees have received courses suited more to the director of the family planning program than to the subordinate personnel. In the subordinate positions the chief demand for expertise is often for statistical analysis in which they usually do some courses, though not at the professional level found in the social science programs. With regard to administration, they frequently find that rather than implement new ideas they must learn more about pre-existing bureaucratic structures and fit in with these.

There are other major questions which our kind of investigation finds difficult to answer. The main one centers on the contribution that the population programs made to the broader outpouring of ideas. Clearly they were centers of excellence from which informed comment could come. Many members of the centers have spoken to us about the attainment of a critical minimum mass as the programs grew and as those involved exchanged ideas with greater numbers of people with varying experiences. The numbers also gave them increased confidence about what they said and wrote. Earlier, those interested in population had often been regarded in the major social science disciplines of the universities as somewhat eccentric and as having an obsession with matters of very marginal concern. The population programs were a source of ideas for journalists and authors who had only passing contact with them. In the United States they made a major input into government instrumentalities and bureaucratic attitudes.

In the national population program best known to the writers, that of Ghana, its establishment depended at every stage on committees, reports and calculations made by persons associated as faculty, students or both with the demography program at the University of Ghana, which had links with the London School of Economics and which was funded by the Population Council and later by the Population

Dynamics Program of the Carolina Population Center. We cannot do justice here to the many Asian programs but some comments can be made in passing. The Taiwan program, centered in the Taiwan Provincial Institute of Family Planning, has the firm support of the Joint Commission on Rural Reconstruction, both of which had strong ties with the University of Michigan's Population Studies Center. The Taichung Project helped convince not only the Taiwan Ministry of Health but also members of the Seoul National University and the Korean Ministry of Health who paid a visit. In Korea the Seoul National University Medical School, through its influence, its alumni, and its journal, was of major importance in shaping the program. In the Philippines, Turkey and Thailand the Governments and administrators paid a great deal of attention to research and teaching centers which had been extensively funded by the Ford Foundation in two cases and the Population Council in the other. In Indonesia the work of the Population Institute at the University of Indonesia and of collaborative research between Indonesian and outside academics was critical in the Government's decision around 1970 to give major emphasis to family planning. The East Asian experience demonstrates almost a Confucianist respect for the scholar. Even in China the philosophy behind the population program shows every sign of originating more from Western university programs than from Marxist literature.[206]

The major problem in evaluating the Foundation's impact on population change is the weight to be placed on the role of the Population Council, especially during its first fifteen years, when Ford money made up almost half its income.

The institutionalization of population programs

Although the creation of university population programs was only an intermediate objective in the Foundation's objectives, any evaluation of the impact of funding must attempt to assess what has been created in universities and what is likely to last. In the social science programs institutionalization is moving quite rapidly. One reason is that they were originally created by university personnel with only a secondary aim of changing the world. Those who sought money were firmly established in the universities and were delighted to have found a funding source which would allow their field of interest to grow. Some sociologists even strengthened their population interests and some demographers paid greater attention to fertility in order to encourage increased funding. Certainly students frequently entered the courses so that they would be supported in a social science program in order to obtain a graduate degree. Other faculty turned their interests towards the Third World, although the evidence is that most did so very willingly, having earlier lacked access or funding.

In the early years there were marked tensions[207] at some universities, especially in departments of sociology. Population specialists often acted in a rather independent way, knowing that they had both funds and possibilities of alternative employment. The growth of demography was felt to threaten the balance of some departments. There were continuous accusations of 'soft science' or of barren empiricism and a belief that funds and ideological convictions about population undermined objective research[208] Often many faculty were on outside funded, non-tenure positions and appeared to spend more time on airplanes than in front of classes of students.

One of the more interesting findings of the present report is the extent to which this situation has changed. During the 1970s most programs decided that their future lay in becoming orthodox disciplinary components of the universities. Even among the greatest enthusiasts for changing the world there was a growing concern with objectivity and with playing a greater role within the university than outside it. Nevertheless, the major gains in academic respectability arose from the effluxion of time. Research projects were completed and publications mounted. Increasingly, other social science disciplines acquired demographic components or population interests. Much had been done to create a new field.[209] Indeed, by the early 1980s demography programs were often seen by universities as an exact study at a time when introspection was growing about the situation and future of the social sciences. The President of Princeton University had seen OPR in this fashion in the mid-1930s and as a concession which might delay the arrival of sociology.

There were substantial losses in this process of institutionalization and gain in respectability. Even those aspects of involvement with the Third World that were less than fully academic did introduce new societies and often provide scholars with experiences that their own institutions could not give them. The non-statistical side of population studies may turn out to be of broader significance for both the social sciences and mankind than statistical demography and an overbalance towards hard science may be damaging in the longer run.

One should not exaggerate the changes that occurred during the 1960s. There was often more of appearance than reality. The work for this report has made it clear to us that only a few senior faculty had continuing research involvement in the Third World. Indeed, many faculty members had their greatest contact before appointment to the programs or to tenured positions and thereafter wrote comparative studies or became primarily involved in research on

American society. Their Third World contacts were mostly with students in their universities and through trips during the summer vacation. Similarly, syllabuses and courses changed less than most of us believed and often resulted in the addition of only one or two extra courses. The largest component with a Third World flavor was student dissertations. Sometimes the program was defeated by the sheer difficulty of entering new areas of ideas. One of the more intriguing threads of the Foundation population involvement was the continuing belief by universities that they should develop economic demography and should have funding to employ the right people. Nearly all now claim that their efforts, although worth making, were far from wholly successful and this sub-discipline still awaits adequate development.

The programs are changing. There is now more emphasis on securing tenured positions from the university than on funding. NICHD core support produces a strange distortion in that renewals depend on the completion and publication of recognized outstanding research projects and hence recruiting must focus primarily on good researchers irrespective of their teaching ability. Foreign students have been declining as a proportion of all students since about 1970 and more attention is now being given to American students and issues. While the Zero Population Growth movement once recruited predominantly male students into the courses, females involved with the Women's Movement or with family planning and abortion interests now tend to be more numerous. Among the disciplines, economists began to show a more lively interest in the population issues around a dozen years ago. However, the fastest growth in interest in recent years has been among anthropologists and coincides with a renewed interest by some demographers in explaining the springs of demographic behavior and the nature of change.

There appears to us to be little doubt that the population programs have become a permanent element of American university social sciences. They are now less concerned with survival than about the type of students they secure and the teaching that would be appropriate. There is little doubt that the American proportion of students will rise as well as the proportion of outside funding for the investigation of American society.

Most American demographers are sociologists while there are fewer economists, statisticians or anthropologists. There remains a strong belief that demography is a specialization of one of these disciplines and there is now a weaker desire to experiment with establishing it in its own right than was the case twelve or fifteen years ago. This is not as strongly the case outside the United States. The Department of Demography of the Australian National University has been a completely separate department for over thirty years. The University of the Philippines plans a departmental structure for population studies. However, the most revolutionary experiment is now occurring at the London School of Economics where a full Department of Population Studies is in the process of being established which will exhibit a three-tier structure with the possibility of taking three successive degrees at the Bachelors, Masters, and Doctoral levels. This was recommended by a committee set up to advise on changes after David Glass's retirement (which then had to take into account his death). The committee was deeply conscious of the LSE record over sixty years and of the work of Carr-Saunders, Kuczynski, Hogben, and Glass. They recommended a reduced emphasis on statistical demography and a greater emphasis in teaching on interrelations with history, economics, and the study of social change.

When this present report was in draft form, we read a paper by Dennis Hodgson, 'Demography as a Social Science and Policy Science,'[210] which deals with aspects of the development of demographic transition theory treated here. More importantly, the treatment of matters just described must be central to our concern because the paper concludes that the atmosphere of technical aid, the availability of money, and the challenge to attempt to change the world meant that the 1950s and 1960s were an aberrant period in scientific demography when social scientists forgot their primary loyalty to their discipline and to understanding the world and attempted to become actors. The paper is a *tour de force* and deserves some comment here, even at the risk of destroying continuity. The paper achieves some of its force by treating changes in ideas as the interaction between a series of American published papers. It underestimates non-American sources such as the impact of Carr-Saunders on Notestein, the effect of teacher upon student as in the case of Willcox upon Notestein, and the march of external events be they censuses or Nehru's announcement of a national population policy for India. We believe it misunderstands the extent to which earlier demographers were willing to offer guidance for action, rather curiously explaining the Indianapolis Study as a detached attempt to analyze the baby boom rather than an effort to discover why American fertility had fallen so low.[211] It fully discusses the danger of commitment to objectivity while completely failing to appreciate the additional understanding that may come from leaving the ivory tower. Certainly, social experimentation can be dangerous but that fact can hardly deny its value for understanding the parameters of demographic behavior.

It is much more difficult to judge the present situation and likely future trends in the population programs in the schools of public health. Such programs, shaped to train cadres, are not rare. They are found in schools of education, administration, and law. However, most of the public health school population programs were less successful than these others in defining whom they were training and for what. Certainly there was a general attitude that they were producing people educated about population matters who could find a role in the population crusade. However, as national family planning programs in Asia became more firmly established, and developed in-service training courses, it became less clear what role foreign trainees in the United States were being prepared for, let alone American trainees. Some of the programs have recently shifted much of the emphasis from family planning administration to health management in recognition of a likely increasing demand in the latter area and of a decline in foreign students.

There is still some debate about standards and the academic focus. We were told repeatedly that social science faculty still regard some of the courses as 'soft science' while many of the faculty of medical schools and even public health schools regard them as unorthodox both in the hetero-geneity of their interests and in their relative lack of concern with sickness and health. The programs have been dominated by Masters degrees and one restriction on a striving for excellence is that few students feel that their training would fit them for the posts that their teachers hold. Often the programs were readily accepted by schools of public health when they attracted a great deal of money, although almost every program has had problems in fighting the schools to retain their own funds.

This is an area where there might be benefit from having only two, or perhaps three, strong programs. The programs have the advantage that the total time spent, at least in the past, by their faculties living in Third World countries and working at village level is vastly greater than that found in most social science population programs. Yet, even the best programs are reluctant to define the product they are pro-ducing and the slots intended for the trainees at the present time, let alone a few years into the future. If the programs are to survive it would appear necessary that this definition should be carried out and also that the usual academic routes should be followed by defining targets of excellence both for students and faculty. It may be pedantic for uni-versities to judge faculty by their specialist contributions to professional books and harshly refereed journals but no other clear way has yet been discovered for maintaining both research and teaching standards.

Introspection about the purposes of these programs is not new. In the late 1960s the Ford Foundation established for three years a mid-career program for bringing bright and clearly capable persons into the field by supporting them for one or two years in public health school population programs. Harkavy wrote to each asking them to share their feelings about their experience. The replies tended to be critical of the programs and often of the whole academic structure. One wrote:

> How does the university mobilize its resources to work on a contemporary social problem? Obviously, the discipline by discipline and parallel departmental structure of universities is not the best mechanism. . . . I wonder what the goal of the program has been as regards your and the Foundation's concept. Is the purpose to train administrators to work primarily in the countries as population advisors? Or, has the purpose been to recruit to the field of population a number of persons with a variety of specialized backgrounds and skills who would then be in a position, after some basic training in population problems, to apply these skills and interests to that field?

Another reported:

> I feel that it is a prodigal waste of time and effort to commit an individual to the type of program available here unless his definite role in the future is one of an administrator of a total family planning program with a qualified staff to assist and advise in all the components thereof. It is my understanding that few of the Fellows here will operate in that capacity and therefore the training they receive, without intending to, is producing, 'jacks of all trades and masters of none' in relation to population. I really would prefer to see the program oriented toward turning out, say, specialists in the educational or the social or the evaluative aspects of family planning programs rather than the broad-spectrumed,

somewhat superficial, products that result from the existing program.

A third wrote:

> Both at the research, and especially at the teaching level the hoped-for integration of many professional disciplines into one comprehensive whole has not been realized. This created some frustrations for me during my academic year. Everyone was talking about the interdisciplinary nature of the population problem, but little of it was illustrated, much less emphasized, in the class rooms.

Another concluded at the end of his course: 'the definition of "population planning" still remains elusive, especially within an academic framework.' Two years earlier David Bell and Francis Sutton had worried in a conference paper that the 'existing centers are not for the most part dealing with the difficult moral, political and scientific questions involved in population policy.'[212]

Outside the United States, the program at Hacettepe University appeared sufficiently well entrenched to survive the storms beginning once again to loom over Turkish universities, and demography had a foothold in other universities in the country. In the Philippines teaching might well be more firmly institutionalized by the Institute being converted to a Department even though some research might be jeopardized. In Egypt the American University in Cairo's Social Research Center would continue to undertake population research as long as externally funded projects were made available but a teaching program was unlikely to develop. It seemed clear that impact on government depended on the research programs, but long-term survival was largely determined by the development of teaching programs.

The unfinished task and the future

The story of population research, theorizing, and the stimulation of large-scale social intervention is a fascinating one and is far from finished. It is only forty years since it was first argued with conviction that global demographic transition was occurring and less than a decade since we began to produce numerical estimates of what the ultimate size of the world's population might be.[213] The first foundation efforts to work on Third World population matters occurred just thirty years ago, while Western Governments entered the arena twenty years ago and international bodies from around 1965. Comprehensive population programs were developed in American universities from around 1960.

The Ford Foundation played a major role in much of this change. Two aspects are particularly noteworthy. The first is the smaller scale but decisive support of the Population Council from 1954. The second is the much larger involvement in population from 1959, and particularly the one-man success story of Oscar Harkavy's funding of the development of university population programs in the early 1960s. It is possible that government would have entered the field in any case a decade later but it is not certain, for the early funding produced an existing structure which was clearly valuable and which would obviously benefit from further financing. Indeed, the movements within the American Government were encouraged by persons in the Foundation's population program and in university programs which had been funded by the programs. Perhaps the most important point is that the later development of population programs with government money would have been both belated and very different. Large teaching programs were urgently needed by 1960, although this was not widely appreciated at the time. Indeed, the need for only a single program was frequently stated. Yet, from the mid-1950s the Population Council Fellowship Program had been demonstrating a lack of specialized programs for fellowship recipients to attend either in the United States or elsewhere. By this time there was also a need for a critical minimum mass of informed opinion on population in the university system and this had not been attained. Furthermore, the critical period in establishing new national population programs in the Third World was in the mid- and latter 1960s and the new university programs were established just in time to meet these needs. Nearly everyone we interviewed spoke of the 1960s as the golden age in the funding of university population programs, quoting less the volume of funds than their flexibility and the extraordinary trust that the Ford Foundation had in the ability of those in universities to spend the money wisely. It may not be surprising that this was appreciated by the recipients. Yet, it is noteworthy that there was remarkable agreement that this lack of enforced direction meant that high-quality and adventurous programs could be quickly erected. Universities are difficult institutions to advise, let alone to induce to create new fields. They trusted this untethered money in a way in which they might not have trusted a large government investment at the time to establish this new field. Over the previous fifteen years the Ford Foundation's Foreign Area and other university social science programs had earned a reputation for seeking quality and this assisted intervention in the more tendentious population field. A hallmark of the intervention in the population area was an emphasis on quality. Both institutions and individuals were sought out that were known to perform outstandingly and to aim at the best. There was a continuing emphasis on funding high-quality research so that research and teaching would at all times be interrelated.

The programs are now being assessed at a time when there is a lull in population interests and when the Ford Foundation no longer funds university-based population programs.

The lull is probably the result of an incorrect assessment of the situation, as will be spelt out below. Certainly, the university programs regard the present period as a crisis more perhaps because they are not certain of the continuation of external funding than because of any particular shortfall at the present time. They do, however, have a feeling of their Third World involvement slipping away from them. The Ford Foundation's reluctance to continue the large-scale funding of population activities is understandable. In real terms its funds have declined and in population they are dwarfed by government expenditure. Furthermore, foundations achieve their impact through innovational audacity and the population area gives the impression of being a firmly established field. Yet it will be suggested below that it may be wise for the Foundation to re-enter the field in a larger way for two reasons. The first is that the problem of swelling human numbers is likely to be with us for at least another century and to be as important a general field during that whole period as public health, agriculture, or medicine. The second reason is that the field already shows a premature hardening of the arteries. Certain kinds of success have been achieved, mostly in Asia, and there is a danger of rigidity in both outlook and research approaches and focusses. There is an urgent need for innovation and change in geographical emphasis. There is also a need for a recovery of the pioneering willingness to work in conditions of adversity where little success can be anticipated in the short term. It is important that the present network of university programs should not be dismantled and that an orientation toward Third World basic research should be maintained.

One of the real perils at the present moment is that there is an appearance of maintaining Third World research links which is not real. The World Fertility Survey has done an excellent job in providing quantitative parameters for current fertility behavior in a wide range of countries (although with a lower density in the areas with which we should begin to concern ourselves more). Nevertheless, many population programs are becoming increasingly concerned with analyzing WFS data tapes in metropolitan universities with, at the most, flying visits to the countries concerned. This is not likely to lead to major research breakthroughs. The fundamental social understandings are just not achieved and the analyses are carried out within a pre-existing mental set. Much of the same can be said of university involvement with many of the AID projects. These are often so strongly oriented toward highly specific goals and toward evaluating action programs that they are inflexible and prevent new areas from being examined. Often their very size, the expense, the number of people involved, and the relation with government means that basic research cannot really be attempted. Important fundamental social science research is often a case of individual or small-scale fumbling by deeply involved and obsessively interested persons living for long periods in the society being studied and having few administrative or advisory functions. The World Fertility Survey analyses are not bringing population programs closer to Third World experience and this is largely true also of the National Academy of Science's National Research Council's study of Population and Demography, although both programs are of great importance for understanding the mechanisms of population trends.

Among the social science population programs we have investigated, a new stability is being achieved although often at some expense to Third World interests. Ironically, it is often their increasing relations with other university departments and a renewed involvement with American and even State affairs which have improved their positions within universities. Three major programs seem to have achieved permanence, safety, and stability. They are those at the University of Michigan, Brown University, and the University of Pennsylvania. All give a major emphasis to teaching and an increasing proportion of their students are assumed to be proceeding to the doctoral degree. The programs at Michigan and Brown have strong anchors in sociology departments. The situation at the University of Pennsylvania is less safe in this regard and much depends on personal relationships although university respect for the present program leadership ensures security for the present time. It will be argued below that a return to area specialization in both research and teaching is urgently needed and the University of Pennsylvania program is unique in that it has in recent years developed a specialization in Africa with funding from the Rockefeller Foundation. At the University of Chicago there is much less certainty about the future of the programs. The Community and Family Studies Center has recently failed to obtain a major hoped-for grant and may well either be phased out or combined in some future amalgamated center. The Population Research and Training Center has lost its original director through retirement and its activities are at least temporarily on the decline. Much will depend on the organizational directions taken by the Faculty of Social Sciences. Princeton University's Office of Population Research is unlikely to develop an increased involvement in doctoral teaching. Its future, like its past, will be largely dependent on first-rate researchers finding adequate funding to pursue major research programs. OPR has always shown great independence in choosing its research projects, and its future work will be very sensitive to the continued availability of such funding. Elsewhere, the University of Texas at Austin will probably continue to receive enough local money to maintain a good Latin American demographic program. Until recently it seemed likely that Georgetown University would grant permission for the development of a doctoral program in demography, which is very much needed in the Washington area, but this hope has now faded. There were other programs which had enjoyed little or no Ford Foundation support. An interesting new program had been revived at Berkeley, University of California, focussing on the economic-demographic interests of Ronald Lee and the anthropological population work of Eugene Hammel. There were also programs with largely American interests at

Duke University and the University of Wisconsin. Economic demography was well entrenched at Yale around Paul Schultz but it was not a training ground for Third World students.

The situation with regard to the population programs in public health schools is more complex. In some ways these programs were more experimental and innovationally interesting. Certainly, they often seem to have had a closer link with Third World reality in that the aggregate period spent in residence in developing countries by their faculty tended to be much greater than that of the social science programs. Usually, however, most of this residence had taken place before joining the program. Indeed, social science faculty had usually pursued fairly orthodox academic careers in American universities while the faculty of the public health programs had enjoyed a much more varied experience. This provides much of the explanation for the lower level of controversy within and about the social science programs, their stricter observance of university practices, and their more rigid adherence to high-standard publication in recognized journals. Nevertheless, in some ways the public health programs maintain a greater atmosphere of reality with regard to the Third World and it is probably important that they should not disappear or be devoted largely to American health management.

Only two programs are solidly entrenched in their universities as major teaching organizations, and even they may not have developed doctoral programs to the extent that their universities will probably come to expect. These two programs are those at Johns Hopkins and Harvard Universities. Both have strengths and weaknesses. The Johns Hopkins program was developed by indisputably respectable public health figures such as Paul Harper and have included as a major feature academically respectable and academically high-quality streams such as reproductive biology and demography, the latter with a surprisingly strong statistical element. However, the program is now in some funding difficulties which arise out of the very nature of the public health

school. Faculty are expected to make a major contribution
to their own salaries from successful grant applications,
and, as the population field changes, the more statistical or
orthodox demographers are experiencing difficulties in doing
this. Harvard remains stable largely because of its endowed
chairs. However, it has experienced some difficulty in obtaining project funding, partly, according to some faculty,
because of their independent and objective attitude to
research. The problem of attracting major social scientists on
the campus, whether sociologists or economists, continues.
The program long remained fairly closely wedded to its basic
Masters degree program although the Ph.D. program has
now come to the fore with a decline in M.A. numbers. The
Center for Population Planning at the University of Michigan
has stabilized, although with faculty in different departments.
As the Taiwan research passes, there seems to be a lessening
in whatever common ground has existed between the two
centers at Michigan. Valuable work is being done at Columbia
University but much depends on the present leadership and
it would be difficult to feel too sanguine about the survival of
the Center for Population and Family Health in a situation
where the University has been willing to provide only one
tenured position. The huge program at the University of North
Carolina is now but a memory, partly perhaps because it was
spread so widely across the campus with the original Center
serving largely as a funding apparatus. Demographers still
work in the Carolina Population Center and courses are
still given in some departments. There has been a major shift
in teaching in the Department of Public Health from family
planning management in the Third World to health care
management in the United States. In no sense does a cohesive
teaching or technical aid program remain.

Even in the early 1960s most programs did not rely for
long solely on Ford Foundation or matching university
money. One of the purposes of Ford Foundation funding
has always been to attract other funds and this was being
successfully achieved by the mid-1960s and massively achieved

by the end of the decade. The fundamental support for most population teaching now comes from the universities and in that sense institutionalization has been achieved. However, the full population programs, and even the caliber of the teaching, depend upon parallel faculty research and on the existence of population centers to serve as a home for both faculty and students. These centers control research finance, fund student scholarships, house research equipment, and provide specialized libraries. Most university libraries are reluctant to invest in runs of Third World census volumes. The support for the centers and associated activities now comes mostly from NICHD. Only some universities have NICHD Center Grants and these can be lost, as was the case with the University of Washington in Seattle, if there is a strategic error in the balance of highly respected research and researchers. Training Grants are somewhat more widely available but they only support American students and tend to abet the turning inward of the interests of population programs. AID money is often plentiful and the gaining or losing of huge specific grants, like that recently obtained by Johns Hopkins' Population Information Program in its School of Hygiene and Public Health, can make or break a program. AID projects still bring Third World students to American population programs but this is a declining interest of such funding. AID projects can bring program faculty in contact with the Third World but usually in a visiting consultant's role rather than as a long-term resident undertaking basic research.

In so far as the gap left by the Ford Foundation is being filled, this is being achieved by the Hewlett and Mellon Foundations, both of which, however, are spending in constant dollars much less money in the population field than the Ford Foundation did. The Hewlett Foundation is consciously filling important areas which looked as if they might be dangerously neglected by Ford's departure and they are financing a considerable number of programs. Their funding objective is narrower and concentrates more exclusively on fertility and family planning but it is flexible and will pay for such precious items as faculty travel to the Third World. However, it will usually not pay salary support for faculty. The Mellon Foundation has provided important support to a few selected programs but the Foundation does not regard social science as being one of its main interests and the present grants may not be evidence of a continuing willingness to support population programs. Both Hewlett and Mellon are willing to have their funds employed to support foreign students. What are becoming increasingly rare are flexible funds to support seed projects to develop proposals for further funding. One reason that population programs are surviving is that a growing shortage of funds and an increasing apprehension about the financial future has forced many of them to struggle harder with their universities for a share of university funds. In the past they often forwent funds on which they rightfully had a claim, partly in order to gain less trammeled freedom. This is no longer the case and presumably this is one of the aims of foundation funding. The cost is often closer work with other departments or closer identification with the whole sociology department in which they are found. There are gains from this and in some universities the population program has been the major cause for increasing respect for the sociology department.

There is probably a widespread misunderstanding of the present situation with regard to population growth. Global population growth rates have not yet been appreciably reduced, that rate having peaked in the 1970s at around 2.2 percent per annum and still being 2.1 percent. The fact that any fall has taken place is explained solely by unexpectedly steep declines in the birth rate in industrialized countries and by the major decline in the Chinese birth rate. What have fallen are the projections of long-term growth. Attention was drawn to this fall by an article by Amy Tsui and Donald Bogue in 1978, 'Declining World Fertility: Trends, Causes, Implications,'[214] and by the subsequent controversy over their conclusions.[215] In point of fact the United Nations

Medium Projection for the year 2000 has fallen only from 6.5 billions to 6.1 billions.[216] Even this contains an assumption that fertility levels in India will continue to fall and that Africa and the Middle East will follow the path already taken by the rest of the world. Optimism comes from declining birth rates in Latin America and in East and Southeast Asia, although it might be noted that the 1983 population growth rates were still 2.3 percent and 1.5 percent respectively in these two regions where sufficient social and economic change has taken place to account for much of the change. Optimism has arisen also from the demonstration that family planning programs have apparently achieved an impact in their own right on the birth rate. Yet, apart from the cases of China and India, notable success has been achieved in Third World Asia only in South Korea, Taiwan, Indonesia, Singapore, Malaysia, and Thailand. The impact of the program as distinct from social change is more debatable in the Philippines, Sri Lanka, and Turkey. What is noteworthy is that many of the countries in the first list are small, totalling 289 millions or 6 percent of world population, and all are East or Southeast Asian. Fertility declines abetted by both social change and family planning programs have also occurred in some small island nations of the Caribbean and the Pacific and Indian Oceans.[217]

There is no evidence that the keys to equal success have yet been found in Africa, the Middle East, or much of South Asia. However, the really precarious basis of the new optimism is found in the cases of India and China. There has been some decline in the Indian birth rate since 1970, possibly from 37 per thousand population in that year to 34 now.[218] However, the 1981 census recorded a higher population than had been anticipated and estimates of the current birth rate now range as high as 37 and of the current rate of population growth as high as 2.2.[219] What has not been widely noted is the fact that much of the fertility decline of the 1970s can be attributed to coercive measures during the Emergency of 1975–77. Those sterilized during that period are increasingly aging out of the reproductive age span and the Indian birth rate has apparently not fallen for several years now.[220] Indeed, it may well rise further. What is also not widely appreciated is that in recent years the Indian Government has regarded its political survival and other political objectives as being more important than the rapid reduction of the birth rate. This is curiously reminiscent of an earlier observation by Frank Notestein that enforced fertility control was more likely to bring down governments than the birth rate. A point of fundamental importance is that it is far from impossible that the Chinese Government will also find itself in a situation where it regards political survival or other political objectives as having priorities above that of its population program. It is already losing some of its leverage over rural populations because of the agricultural reforms and it seems likely that the Chinese birth rate will be higher at the end of this decade than it is now.

The central point is that we still know practically nothing about reducing fertility levels in Africa, the Middle East, and much of South Asia. Among the indigenous population of mainland Africa fertility has definitely been reduced in only one country, Tunisia. This is not because of a failure to experiment with national family planning programs for these have existed in Egypt, Morocco, Ghana, and Kenya while there have also been programs in countries like Botswana and considerable support for family planning activities in Tanzania and parts of Nigeria. For some years the birth rate declined in Egypt, but it subsequently rose again to its original height and it is not yet clear that the fall has been renewed.[221] The Kenya Family Planning Program has been limited by consumer demand and its seventeen years of operation have witnessed no decline in the birth rate and a rise in the rate of natural increase to a record 4 percent per annum. Rising incomes in the Middle East and North Africa have astonishingly had no impact on the birth rate so far. Pakistan and Bangladesh have experienced a family planning program going back a quarter of a century, the world's second oldest national program, but birth rates are still around 50 per thousand with no convincing evidence of decline.

The point being made here is not that fertility control in these areas is impossible but that we have been misled by programs in a very specific part of Asia where there is a strong tradition of national leadership and where state morality can easily become individual morality. This is not true in the Moslem heartland stretching from Mauritania to Bangladesh. Nor is it true south of the Sahara where the nation state has no ancient tradition and where fear of sterility, even as measured by the cessation of child-bearing, lies deep in the culture. Much yet remains to be understood about the implication of women's position in the Middle East. The answer in all these areas is clearly not just better administered family planning programs and the teaching of lessons from South Korea and Taiwan. The fundamental need is for guidance from small-scale experimental family planning projects and from a much greater knowledge of the social and economic contexts of reproduction. Small-scale studies have begun,[222] but vastly more work is needed. We need either to bring in the anthropologists and area cultural specialists or to adopt their methods. We need long-term and collaborative studies of the context of reproduction undertaken by methods other than surveys. In Africa and elsewhere there should be continuing population research institutions such as the Rhodes Livingston Institute once provided for anthropologists or the British Medical Research Council has provided for health workers in Gambia. We may be able to produce reproductive equivalents of the *American Dilemma.*[223]

Work of this kind is of critical importance and is innovative. It is likely to be difficult and in the short term unrewarding. It is not likely to appeal to governments or to receive easily government funding. There appears to us to be an area here of transcending importance with a major claim on future Ford Foundation funding. This implies that it will be necessary to keep together the university base for population studies in the developed world. Nevertheless, any future emphasis must be on basic research in the developing world, especially in the great arc from Botswana to Burma, undertaken by the best social scientists whatever their cultural origins. This does not necessarily mean an invasion of foreigners because local social scientists should know their cultures best, provided that they have not been trained to see demographic and reproductive phenomena with foreign eyes.

The Ford Foundation achievement in population has been remarkable. The establishment of the population centers provided the major anchor for contemporary social demography. There may be a greater achievement still to come. The future achievement may again lie more in the social scientific than in the biomedical field. The pill is still regarded as unsatisfactory in India and the IUD in much of the Middle East, yet new technological breakthroughs may be outpaced by social change.

The population debate is likely to flare up again, perhaps taking older forms rather than more recent ones. It seems doubtful that the major stress will again be laid on the interrelation between the rate of population increase and that of economic growth at either the national or individual level, as was the case in the late 1950s and the 1960s. Growth seems to depend on such a welter of factors, including political and social ones. However, there is increasing evidence that, as we approach a ceiling, slow-growing global population of whatever size—8 billions, 10 billions, or 12 billions—there will be intensified discussion about the world's ability to provide a reasonable standard of living and diet for these numbers. The debate will not be strictly Malthusian because it will center on questions of minimum needs and comfortable standards of living rather than on dietary levels where health and life itself are threatened. A recent contribution to that debate argues that adequate per capita consumption levels (employing a measure based on plant food but allowing those with low meat diets to increase their meat consumption) are around 50 percent higher than the present world average but 40 percent lower than that now found in North America, Australia, New Zealand, Argentina, and France.[224] The author argues that the adequate diet he has defined could not be provided for more than 7.5 billions, a population likely to be reached before the year 2020, according to the medium variant of the latest United Nations projections and eventually to be exceeded (although not by a large margin) by the low variant.[225] The authors' view is that we are, nevertheless, likely to follow the path of the medium variant, to a ceiling of about 11 billions, on about today's dietary levels, and then reduce numbers as the only way of improving the lot of the poor (presumably through market mechanisms as much as by international decision). If such viewpoints gain a measure of agreement, then the debate will return in the immediate future to growth levels and what ceilings they portend.

Notes

1. Richard Magat, *The Ford Foundation at Work: Philanthropic Choices, Methods and Styles*, Plenum Press, New York, 1979, pp. 93–4.
2. United Nations Department of Social Affairs Population Bulletin No. 1, December 1951; United Nations, *Proceedings of the World Population Conference, 1954, Papers*, III, 1954, pp. 283–328. United Nations Department of Economic and Social Affairs, *Population Studies*: No. 28, 1958; No. 41, 1966; No. 53, 1973; No. 60, 1977; United Nations, Department of International Economic and Social Affairs, *Population Studies*, No. 82, 1982. All published at United Nations, New York.
3. John C. Caldwell, 'The containment of world population growth,' *Studies in Family Planning*, 6(12), December 1975, pp. 429–36. (Reprint of a paper presented in the opening session of the Tribune, World Population Conference, Bucharest, August 1974.)
4. Extension of projections published in United Nations Department of International Economic and Social Affairs, *Demographic Indicators of Countries: Estimates and projections as assessed in 1980*, ST/ESA/SER.A/82, United Nations, New York, 1982.
5. United Nations, 1954, op. cit.
6. G. H. Knibbs, *The Mathematical Theory of Population, of its Character and Fluctuations, and of the Factors which Influence Them*, Appendix A of the 1911 Census of Australia, 1, Australian Government, Melbourne, 1917, pp. 30–3.
7. Ibid., p. 33.
8. W. R. Crocker, *The Japanese Population Problem: The Coming Crisis*, Allen and Unwin, London, 1931.
9. William F. Willcox (ed.), *International Migrations, 2, Interpretations*, National Bureau of Economic Research, Publication No. 18, New York, 1931, pp. 42, 43, and 78.
10. Ibid., p. 79.
11. Raymond Pearl, *The Natural History of Population*, Oxford University Press, London, 1939, p. 257.

12. Raymond Pearl, *Studies in Human Biology*, Williams and Wilkins, Baltimore, 1924.

13. See D. V. Glass, *Population Policies and Movement in Europe*, Clarendon Press, Oxford, 1940, Appendix; A. L. Bowley, 'Births and population of Great Britain,' *The Journal of the Royal Economic Society*, 34, 1924, pp. 188–92.

14. P. K. Whelpton, 'Population of the United States, 1925–1975,' *The American Journal of Sociology*, 34(2), September 1928, pp. 253–70.

15. Warren S. Thompson and P. K. Whelpton, *Population Trends in the United States*, McGraw-Hill, New York, 1933.

16. The KAP Survey (largely promoted by the Population Council and owing its name to a suggestion by John Kantner to Bernard Berelson) attempted to determine the extent of family planning knowledge, attitudes, and practice in a community, region, or country. Cf. John C. Caldwell *et al.*, *A Manual for Surveys of Fertility and Family Planning: Knowledge, Attitudes, and Practice*, The Population Council, New York, 1970.

17. The World Fertility Survey (WFS) was, from 1972 to 1983, an international research program whose purpose was to assess the current state of human fertility throughout the world. This was done principally through promoting and supporting nationally representative, internationally comparable, and scientifically designed and conducted sample surveys of fertility behavior in as many countries as possible (sixty-two in 1981). It was funded by UNFPA, AID, and a number of other government technical aid organizations.

18. *The Declining Birth-Rate: Its Causes and Effects (Being the Report of and the chief evidence taken by the National Birth-Rate Commission, instituted, with official recognition, by the National Council of Public Morals—for the Promotion of Race Regeneration—Spiritual, Moral and Physical)* (2nd edn), Chapman and Hall, London, 1917, p. 21, reporting on the results of a survey of women who had received a college education and some of their female relatives.

19. For instance, T. A. Coghlan, *The Decline in the Birth-Rate of New South Wales and other Phenomena of Child-Birth*, Government Printer, Sydney, 1903, p. 68.

20. For instance, New South Wales, *Royal Commission on the Decline of the Birth-Rate and on the Mortality of Infants in New*

South Wales, Government Printer, Sydney, 1904; Neville Hicks, *'This Sin and Scandal': Australia's Population Debate 1891-1911*, Australian National University Press, Canberra, 1978.

21. Coghlan, op. cit., p. 68.

22. Frank Lorimer and Frederick Osborn, *Dynamics of Population*, Macmillan, New York, 1934, pp. 273-5.

23. Robert S. Lynd and Helen Merrell Lynd, *Middletown: A Study in American Culture*, Harcourt, Brace and Co., New York, 1929, p. 23.

24. Raymond Pearl, 'Contraception and fertility in 4945 married women. A second report on a study of family limitation,' *Human Biology*, 6, 1934, pp. 335-401; Pearl, 1939, op. cit.

25. Regina Stix and Frank Notestein, 'Effectiveness of birth control,' *Milbank Memorial Fund Quarterly*, 12(1), January 1934, pp. 57-68, and *Controlled Fertility: An Evaluation of Clinic Service*, Williams and Wilkins, Baltimore, 1940.

26. For the 1902-11 marriage cohort this was 70 percent (ibid., p. 52).

27. Norman Himes, *The Medical History of Contraception*, Williams and Wilkins, Baltimore, 1936.

28. E. Lewis-Faning, *Report on an Enquiry into Family Limitation and Its Influence on Human Fertility during the Past Fifty Years* (Papers of the Royal Commission on Population, 1), HMSO, London, 1949, p. 52.

29. Paul Demeny, 'Observations on population policy and population program in Bangladesh,' *Population and Development Review*, 1(2), December 1975, pp. 307-21.

30. P. K. Whelpton and C. V. Kiser (eds), *Social and Psychological Factors Affecting Fertility*, I-V, Milbank Memorial Fund, New York, 1946, 1950, 1952, 1954, 1958.

31. A summary of the papers may be found in Edgar Schuster, 'The First International Eugenics Congress,' *Eugenics Review*, 4(3), October 1912, pp. 223-56.

32. Margaret Sanger (ed.), *Proceedings of the World Population Conference 1927*, Edward Arnold, London, 1927.

33. Kenneth M. Ludmerer, *Genetics and American Society: A Historical Appraisal*, Johns Hopkins University Press, Baltimore, 1972, p. 95.

34. Walter F. Willcox, 'The nature and significance of the changes in the birth and death rates in recent years,' *American Statistical Association*, New Series, No. 113, March 1916, p. 14.

35. Sanger, op. cit., p. 5.
36. E. M. East, 'Food and population' in Sanger (ed.), op. cit., pp. 85–92.
37. E. A. Ross, *Standing Room Only?*, Century Co., New York, 1927.
38. George Handley Knibbs, *The Shadow of the World's Future or the Earth's Population Possibilities and the Consequences of the Present Rate of Increase of the Earth's Inhabitants*, Ernest Benn, London, 1928.
39. A. M. Carr-Saunders, *The Population Problem: A Study in Human Evolution*, Clarendon, Oxford, 1922.
40. Census of India, *Census Report*, 1921.
41. A. M. Carr-Saunders, *World Population: Past Growth and Present Trends*, Frank Cass, London, 1936.
42. Robert R. Kuczynski, *The Balance of Births and Deaths:* 1, *Western and Northern Europe*, Macmillan, New York, 1928 and 2, *Eastern and Southern Europe*, Brookings Institute, Washington, 1931.
43. *Milbank Memorial Fund Quarterly Bulletin,* 8(4), October 1930, pp. 97–108; Chi-Ming Chiao, 'A Study of the Chinese Population,' (in 4 instalments), *Milbank Memorial Fund Quarterly Bulletin,* 11(4), October 1933, pp. 325–41; *Milbank Memorial Fund Quarterly,* 12(1), January 1934, pp. 85–96; 12(2), April 1934, pp. 171–83; 12(3), July 1934, pp. 270–82.
44. Frank W. Notestein, 'A demographic study of 38,256 rural families in China,' *Milbank Memorial Fund Quarterly,* 16(1), January 1938, pp. 57–79.
45. E. F. Penrose, *Population Theories and their Application with Special Reference to Japan*, Food Research Institute, Stanford University (Stanford), 1934, pp. 119–20.
46. W. Wendell Cleland, *The Population Problem in Egypt*, Science Press, Lancaster, Penn., 1936.
47. W. Wendell Cleland, 'A population plan for Egypt,' *Milbank Memorial Fund Quarterly,* 22(4), October 1944, pp. 409–23.
48. Frank W. Notestein *et al., The Future Population of Europe and the Soviet Union*, League of Nations, Geneva, 1944, p. 3.
49. Notestein *et al.,* op. cit.; Wilbert E. Moore, *Economic Demography of Eastern and Southern Europe*, Economic, Financial and Transit Department, League of Nations, Geneva, 1945; Frank Lorimer, *The Population of the Soviet Union: History*

and Prospects, Economic, Financial and Transit Department, League of Nations, Geneva, 1946; Dudley Kirk, *Europe's Population in the Interwar Years*, Economic, Financial and Transit Department, League of Nations, Geneva, 1946.

50. Frank W. Notestein, 'Some applications of population change for post-war Europe,' (Read February 19, 1943), *Proceedings of the American Philosophical Society*, 87(2), August 1943, pp. 165–74.

51. Frank W. Notestein, 'Foreword' to Irene B. Taeuber, *The Population of Japan*, Princeton University Press, Princeton, 1958; Frank W. Notestein, 'Foreword' to Kingsley David, *The Population of India and Pakistan*, Princeton University Press, Princeton, 1951.

52. Taeuber, op. cit.; Davis, op. cit.

53. George W. Barclay, *Colonial Development and Population in Taiwan*, Princeton University Press, Princeton, 1954; T. E. Smith, *Population Growth in Malaya: An Analysis of Recent Trends*, Royal Institute of International Affairs, London, 1952.

54. Dudley Kirk, 'Population changes and the postwar world,' *American Sociological Review*, 9(1), February 1944, pp. 28–35.

55. Irene B. Taeuber and Edwin G. Beal, 'The dynamics of population in Japan,' *Milbank Memorial Fund Quarterly*, 22(3), July 1944, pp. 222–25; Kingsley Davis, 'Demographic fact and policy in India,' *Milbank Memorial Fund Quarterly*, 22(3), July 1944, pp. 256–78; Wilbert E. Moore, 'Agricultural population and rural economy in Eastern and Southern Europe,' *Milbank Memorial Fund Quarterly*, 22(3), July 1944, pp. 279–99; Ernest Jurkat, 'Prospects for population growth in the Near East,' *Milbank Memorial Fund Quarterly*, 22(3), July 1944, pp. 300–17; Clyde V. Kiser, 'The demographic position of Egypt,' *Milbank Memorial Fund Quarterly*, 22(4), October 1944, pp. 383–408; W. Wendell Cleland, 'A population plan for Egypt,' *Milbank Memorial Fund Quarterly*, 22(4), October 1944, pp. 409–23; Frank W. Notestein, 'Problems of policy in relation to areas of heavy population pressure,' *Milbank Memorial Fund Quarterly*, 22(4), October 1944, pp. 424–44.

56. Warren S. Thompson, *Population and Peace in the Pacific*, University of Chicago Press, Chicago, 1946, pp. 101 and 103.

57. Davis, 1944, op. cit.

58. Notestein, 1943, op. cit., p. 174.

59. Frank W. Notestein, 'Population: the long view,' in Theodore Schultz (ed.), *Food for the World*, University of Chicago Press, Chicago, 1945, pp. 36–57.

60. 'Observations of participants', in Schultz (ed.), op. cit., p. 210.

61. Ibid., p. 211.

62. Thompson, op. cit., pp. 33 ff.

63. Kingsley Davis, 'Human fertility in India,' *American Journal of Sociology*, 52(3), November 1946, p. 254.

64. C. P.Blacker, 'Stages in population growth,' *Eugenics Review*, 39(3), 1947, pp. 88–102.

65. Ibid., p. 99.

66. 'Preface' to the English edition of William Vogt, *Road to Survival*, Victor Gollancz, London, 1949.

67. Ibid., p. 237.

68. Ibid., p. 280.

69. Marshall C. Balfour, Roger F. Evans, Frank W. Notestein, and Irene B. Taeuber, *Public Health and Demography in the Far East: Report of a Survey Trip, September 13–December 13, 1948*, The Rockefeller Foundation, New York, 1950.

70. Raymond B. Fosdick, *The Story of the Rockefeller Foundation*, Harper and Brothers, New York, 1952, pp. 80 ff.

71. Ibid., p. 222.

72. Balfour *et al.*, op. cit., p. 6.

73. Ibid., p. 8.

74. Ibid., p. 9.

75. Ibid., pp. 34–6.

76. Ibid., p. 112.

77. Ibid.

78. Ibid., p. 83.

79. Ibid., pp. 119–20.

80. Henry Ford II, 'Preface' to The Study Committee (under the chairmanship of H. Rowan Gaither, jun.), *Report of the Study for the Ford Foundation on Policy and Program*, p. 9.

81. Ibid., p. 14.

82. Irene B. Taeuber, 'Ceylon as a demographic laboratory: preface to analysis,' *Population Index*, 15(4), October 1949, pp. 293–304; Barclay, op. cit.; J. Mayone Stycos, *Family and Fertility in Puerto Rico: A Study of the Lower Income Group*, Columbia University Press, New York, 1955; United Nations *Demographic Yearbook 1957*, United Nations, New York, 1957.

83. Kiser, 1944, op. cit., p. 406
84. Davis, 1944, op. cit., p. 276.
85. Notestein, 1945, op. cit., p. 57.
86. Irene B. Taeuber, 'Literature on future populations, 1943-48,' *Population Index*, 15(1), January 1949, p. 8.
87. United Nations, 1982, op. cit.
88. United Nations, *World Economic Report, 1948.*
89. United Nations, Department of Social Affairs, *World Population Trends 1920-1947*, ST/SOA/Series A. Population Studies, No. 3, United Nations, New York, 1949.
90. United Nations, Department of Social Affairs, Population Division, *Population Bulletin, No. 1—December 1951*, ST/SOA/Ser.N/1., United Nations, New York, 1951.
91. See the sources cited in Note 2.
92. Paul K. Hatt, *Backgrounds of Human Fertility in Puerto Rico*, Princeton University Press, Princeton, 1952.
93. Stycos, op. cit.
94. Frank W. Notestein, 'Economic problems of population change,' in *8th International Conference of Agricultural Economists, 1952*, Oxford University Press, London, 1953.
95. Frank W. Notestein, 'Policy of the Indian Government on family limitation,' *Population Index*, 17(4), October 1951, pp. 254-63.
96. But note Frank Notestein, 'Keeping PAA professionally pure,' *P.A.A. Affairs*, Summer 1983, 3 (excerpt from Notestein's 'Reminiscences . . .,' *Milbank Memorial Fund Quarterly*, 49(4), Pt.2, October 1971, pp. 67-84).
97. This section is drawn from interviews over two decades (beginning with Frank Lorimer in 1964) but draws heavily on interviews with Frank Notestein and Ansley Coale in January 1983.
98. Notestein, 1953, op. cit.
99. Irene B. Taeuber and Marshall C. Balfour, 'The control of fertility in Japan,' *Approaches to Problems of High Fertility in Japan*, Milbank Memorial Fund, New York, 1952, pp. 102-28.
100. Wilbert E. Moore, *Industrialization and Labor: Social Aspects of Economic Development* (published for the Institute of World Affairs, New School of Social Research), Cornell University Press, Ithaca, 1951.
101. Kingsley Davis, 'Fertility control and the demographic transition in India,' *The Interrelations of Demographic, Economic and Social Problems in Selected Underdeveloped Areas*, 1953 Milbank

Memorial Fund Round Table paper, *Milbank Memorial Fund Quarterly*, New York, 1954, p. 66.

102. Frank Lorimer, *Culture and Human Fertility*, UNESCO, Paris, 1954, p. 250.

103. United Nations Department of Social Affairs Population Division, *The Determinants and Consequences of Population Trends*, Population Studies, No. 17, ST/SOA/Ser.A/17, United Nations, New York, 1953.

104. United Nations, *Proceedings of the World Population Conference, 1954, Rome, 31 August–10 September 1954, Papers*, E/CONF.13/415, United Nations, New York (1955). United Nations, Proceedings of the World Population Conference, 1954, Summary Report, E/CONF.13/412, United Nations, New York, 1955.

105. United Nations, *Seminar on Population in Asia and the Far East, Bandung, Indonesia, 21 November–3 December 1955, Report* and *Working Papers*, Bandung, 1955. Also interviews with Dudley Kirk and R. M. Sundrum.

106. Julian L. Simon, *The Ultimate Resource*, Princeton University Press, Princeton, 1981.

107. Richard R. Nelson, 'A theory of the low-level equilibrium trap in underdeveloped economies,' *American Economic Review*, 46(5), December 1956, pp. 894–908.

108. Harvey Leibenstein, *Economic Backwardness and Economic Growth: Studies in the Theory of Economic Development*, Wiley, New York, 1957.

109. Ansley J. Coale and Edgar Hoover, *Population Growth and Development in Low-Income Countries*, Princeton University Press, Princeton, 1958.

110. *The New York Times*, 8 March 1959.

111. Judith Blake Davis, in collaboration with J. Mayone Stycos and Kingsley Davis, *Family Structure in Jamaica*, The Free Press, Glencoe, 1961.

112. J. Mayone Stycos and Kurt W. Back, *The Control of Human Fertility in Jamaica*, Cornell University Press, Ithaca, 1964.

113. United Nations Department of Economic and Social Affairs, *The Mysore Population Study*, Population Studies No. 34, ST/SOA/Series A/34, United Nations, New York, 1961.

114. Philip M. Hauser and Otis Dudley Duncan, *The Study of Population: An Inventory and Appraisal*, University of Chicago Press, 1959.

115. The Study Committee, *Report . . .*, op. cit.

116. Magat, op. cit., pp. 18–19.

117. Ibid., p. 19.

118. Ibid., p. 30.

119. Francis Sutton, 'The role of foundations in development,' Speech delivered at Texas A & M University, Friday, September 19, 1980.

120. Notestein, 1953, op. cit.

121. Magat, op. cit., p. 31.

122. J. T. Marten, *Census of India, 1921,* 1—*India*, Part 1—*Report*, Superintendent of Government Printing, Government of India, Calcutta, 1924, pp. 48–9.

123. Carr-Saunders, 1922, op. cit.

124. J. H. Hutton, *Census of India, 1931,* 1—*India* Part 1—*Report*, Manager of Publications, Government of India, Delhi, 1933, pp. 31–2.

125. A. E. Porter, Appendix to Chap. 1, ibid.

126. Pyare Kishan Wattal, *The Population Problem in India: A Census Study*, Bennett, Coleman & Co., Bombay, 1916.

127. Notes from interviews with Lady Rama Rao, 1968–69 project.

128. Warren Thompson, *Population Problems*, McGraw-Hill, New York, 1930.

129. Carr-Saunders, 1936, op. cit.

130. S. Chandrasekhar, *India's Population: Fact and Policy*, Asia Press Book, John Day, New York, 1946, pp. 86 ff.

131. Margaret Sanger, *An Autobiography*, Norton, New York, 1938, p. 461.

132. India Famine Inquiry Commission, *Final Report*, Government Press, Madras, 1945, pp. 385–6.

133. India. Health Survey and Development Committee. *Report of the Health Survey and Development Committee,* II, *Recommendations*, Manager, Government of India Press, Delhi, 1946, pp. 483–7.

134. Davis, 1944, op. cit.

135. K. T. Shah (ed.), *Population*, Report of the Population Sub-Committee of the National Planning Committee, Vora and Co., Bombay, 1947.

136. Ibid., p. 14.

137. Ibid., p. 113.

174   *Notes*

138. Interviews with R. A. Gopalaswami and C. Chandrasekaran; Notestein, 1951, op. cit.

139. Committee documents in the possession of C. Chandrasekaran.

140. Notestein, 1951, op. cit.

141. R. A. Gopalaswami, 'Reprint from "Census of India, 1951, Volume I, India, Part I-A Report" ' (pp. 177–91). Chap. V, 'The Prospect—1981. Future growth of population' in *Proceedings of the World Population Conference, 1954, Rome, 31 August–10 September 1954, Papers*, III, pp. 173–89.

142. Cf. Agricultural Production Team, Report on *India's Food Crisis and Steps to Meet It*, Government of India, Delhi, 1959.

143. Edwin Driver, *Differential Fertility in Central India*, Princeton University Press, Princeton, 1963.

144. Leona Baumgartner and Frank W. Notestein, Mission Report: 'Suggestions for a Practical Program of Family Planning and Child Care', submitted December 1955 to Rajkumari Amrit Kaur, pp. 15–16.

145. Population Branch, Bureau of Social Affairs of the United Nations, 'Proposed Regional Centre for Demographic Research and Training,' *Seminar on Population in Asia and the Far East, Bandung, Indonesia, 21 November–3 December 1955*, Working Paper B–21, New York, November 1955, p. 2.

146. United Nations, 'Report,' *Seminar on Population in Asia and the Far East, Bandung, Indonesia, 21 November–3 December, 1955*, Bandung, December 1955, p. 25.

147. Asha A. Bhende, Tara Kanitkar, and G. Rama Rao, *Seventeen Years of I.I.P.S.*, International Institute for Population Studies, Bombay, 1976, pp. 3–4.

148. Memo from Bernard Berelson after talks with John Durand, Director, Population Branch, 21 December 1956.

149. Dorothy Campbell and Wendy Cosford, 'Population Policies and Programmes Projects,' Department of Demography, Australian National University, Canberra, 1971–2, 46, quoting *The Times*, London.

150. Ibid., p. 174.

151. Ibid., p. 177.

152. Jeanne Clare Ridley, 'The 1901–1910 low fertility cohorts in the United States: Fecundity and family planning,' Seminar Paper, Department of Demography, Australian National University, Canberra, 24 May 1983; for closely comparable Australian data,

see John C. Caldwell, 'Fertility control,' in United Nations Economic and Social Commission for Asia and the Pacific, *Population of Australia*, Country Monograph Series No. 9, United Nations, New York, 1982, pp. 230-58.

153. For Australia, 1971 Melbourne Survey of the Department of Demography, Australian National University; for the United States, Charles F. Westoff and Larry Bumpass, 'The revolution in birth control practices of U.S. Roman Catholics,' *Science*, **179** (4068), 5 January 1973, pp. 41-4.

154. David E. Bell and Francis X. Sutton, Paper at Conference of Ford Regional Representatives, Lake Como, 1967, pp. 2-4.

155. Sutton, op. cit., p. 13.

156. Ibid., pp. 7-8.

157. Margat, op. cit., pp. 103-6.

158. Ibid., pp. 97-9.

159. Bernard Berelson and Ronald Freedman, 'A study in fertility control,' *Scientific American*, **210** (May 1964), pp. 29-37.

160. Ronald Freedman and John Y. Takeshita (eds), *Family Planning in Taiwan: An Experiment in Social Change*, Princeton University Press, Princeton, 1969.

161. Malaysia. National Family Planning Board. *Report on West Malaysian Family Survey 1966-1967*, Kuala Lumpur (1968).

162. Evidence collected in the 1968-69 Asian Population Policy Project.

163. The Oxford and Cambridge model, in which teaching took place in the colleges rather than the university, was not considered appropriate for the colonies. Eric Ashby, *Universities: British, Indian, African*, Weidenfeld and Nicolson, London, 1966, pp. 19-22.

164. Fosdick, op. cit., pp. 42 and 96 ff.

165. John B. Wyon and John E. Gordon, *The Khanna Study: Population Problems in the Rural Punjab*, Harvard University Press, Cambridge, 1971.

166. Freedman and Takeshita, op. cit.

167. Bhasker D. Misra, Ali Ashraf, Ruth Simmons, and George B. Simmons, *Organization for Change: A System Analysis of Family Planning in Rural India*, Center for South and Southeast Asian Studies, The University of Michigan in co-operation with the Family Planning Foundation of India (Michigan Papers in South and Southeast Asia, No. 21), 1982.

168. In the following sections, use has been made of: Philip R. Lee, 'The development of federal policies related to population prob-

lems,' in Daniel O. Price (ed.), *The 99th Hour: The Population Crisis in the United States*, The University of North Carolina Press, Chapel Hill, 1967, pp. 84–94; Philip R. Lee, 'The roles of government agencies' in Mary Steichen Calderone (ed.), *Manual of Family Planning and Contraceptive Practice*, Williams and Wilkins, Baltimore, 2nd edn, 1970, pp. 74–82.

169. Bernard Berelson *et al.* (eds), *Family Planning and Population Programs: A Review of World Developments*, University of Chicago Press, Chicago, 1966.

170. United Nations, *World Population Conference, 1965*, E/CONF.41/2, United Nations, New York, 1966, 4 vols.

171. Oscar Harkavy, in collaboration with Frederick S. Jaffe and Samuel M. Wishik, 'Implementing DHEW Policy on Family Planning and Population,' September 1967, mimeo, p. 9.

172. Anna L. Southam and Oscar Harkavy, 'Resources for research in reproductive biology,' Attachment C, ibid.

173. Office of Technology Assessment, *World Population and Fertility Planning Technologies: The Next 20 Years*, Congress of the United States, Washington, 1981, p. 107.

174. Panel on Fertility Determinants, Committee on Population and Demography, Commission on Behavioral and Social Sciences and Education, National Research Council, *Reports*, National Academy Press, Washington, various dates from 1980.

175. *Studies in Family Planning*, No. 16, January 1967; the heads of state were: Dr Carlos Lleras Restrepo, President of Colombia; Dr D. Urho Kekkonen, President of Finland; Mrs Indira Gandhi, Prime Minister of India; General Chung Hee Park, President of the Republic of Korea; Tunku Abdul Rahman, Prime Minister of Malaysia; His Majesty King Hassan II of Morocco; His Majesty King Mahendra of Nepal; Lee Kwan Yew, Prime Minister of Singapore; Tage Erlander, Prime Minister of Sweden; Habib Bourguiba, President of Tunisia; Gamal Abdel Nasser, President of the United Arab Republic; Marshal Josip Broz-Tito, President of Yugoslavia.

176. Saad Gadalla, *Is There Hope? Fertility and Family Planning in a Rural Egyptian Community*, The Social Research Center, The American University in Cairo Press and The Carolina Population Center, The University of North Carolina at Chapel Hill, Cairo and Chapel Hill, 1978.

177. Turgut Metiner, 'Turkey,' in Berelson (ed.), op. cit., pp. 135–41.

178. Committee on Population and Demography, National Research Council, *Trends in Fertility and Mortality in Turkey, 1935–1975*, Report No. 8, National Academy Press, Washington, 1982.

179. Nathan Keyfitz and Widjojo Nitisastro, *Soal penduduk dan pembanguan Indonesia* (The problem of population and development in Indonesia), Pembangunan, Jakarta, 1954.

180. Peter McDonald, *'Demografi Teknik,'* mimeo.

181. Coale and Hoover, op. cit.

182. Sidney Goldstein, Pichit Pitaktepsombati and Alice Goldstein, 'Migration to urban places in Thailand: Interrelations among origin, recency, frequency and motivations.' Paper no. 21. Chulalongkorn University, Institute of Population Studies, Bangkok, 1977.

183. Giorgio Mortara, 'Contributions of the Brazilian Institute of Geography and Statistics to population studies, 1936–1951,' *Bulletin of the International Statistical Institute*, 33(4), 1954, pp. 175–90.

184. Jorge Balan, Harley L. Browning, and Elizabeth Jelin, *Men in a Developing Society: Geographic and Social Mobility in Monterrey, Mexico*, University of Texas Press for Institute of Latin American Studies, Austin, 1973.

185. Robert W. Hodge and Mary M. Kritz, 'Evaluation Report of the Population and Development Policy Research Program jointly sponsored by The Rockefeller Foundation and the Ford Foundation,' October 1978, mimeo.

186. Sidney Goldstein, 'Report on Ford–Rockefeller Population and Development Policy Research Program,' September 1977, mimeo.

187. Samir Amin, 'Underdevelopment and dependence in Black Africa,' *Journal of Modern African Studies*, 10(4), 1972, pp. 503–24, Samir Amin, *Neo-Colonialism in West Africa*, Penguin, London, 1973.

188. Kingsley Davis, 'Population policy: Will current programs succeed?' *Science*, 158(3802), pp. 730–9, November 10, 1967.

189. Paul R. Ehrlich, *The Population Bomb*, Ballantine Books, New York, 1968.

190. Donella H. Meadows *et al.*, *The Limits to Growth: A report for the Club of Rome's project on the predicament of mankind*, Universe (for Potomac Associates), New York, 1972.

191. John D. Rockefeller III, 'Population growth: the role of the

developed world,' International Union for the Scientific Study of Population, *Lecture Series on Population*, Liège, 1974.

192. W. Parker Mauldin, Nazli Choucri, Frank W. Notestein, and Michael Teitelbaum, 'A Report on Bucharest: The World Population Conference and The Population Tribune, August 1974,' *Studies in Family Planning*, 5(12), December 1974, pp. 357–95.

193. U.S. Commission on Population Growth and the American Future, *Population and the American Future: The Report of the Commission on Population Growth and the American Future*, Government Printing Office, Washington, 1972.

194. Coale and Hoover, op. cit.

195. Simon, op. cit.

196. Nick Eberstadt, *'Population Control' and the Wealth of Nations: The Implications for American Policy*, Department of State, United States Government, Washington, 1981.

197. E.g. *International Family Planning Perspectives.*

198. *The New York Times*, January 24, 1983, Section A, p. 18.

199. On threshold theory, see the *Population Bulletin* of the United Nations, No. 7—1963, ST/SOA/Ser.N/7. On Latin America, see Frank W. Oechsli and Dudley Kirk, 'Modernization and the demographic transition in Latin America and the Caribbean,' *Economic Development and Cultural Change*, 23(3), April 1975, pp. 391–419, but note qualifications in John C. Caldwell, 'Toward a restatement of demographic transition theory,' *Population and Development Review*, 2(3 and 4), September and December 1976, p. 333.

200. Susan Hill Cochrane, *Fertility and Education: What Do We Really Know?* World Bank Staff Occasional Papers Number 26, published for the World Bank by The Johns Hopkins University Press, Baltimore, 1979; Harvey J. Graff, 'Literacy, education, and fertility, past and present: A critical review,' *Population and Development Review*, 5(1), March 1979, pp. 105–40; John C. Caldwell, 'Mass education as a determinant of the timing of fertility decline,' *Population and Development Review*, 6(2), June 1980, pp. 225–55.

201. John C. Caldwell: as a research scholar of the Australian National University and with ECAFE (now ESCAP) in Thailand in 1959 and in Malaysia in 1960; at the University of Ghana with Population Council support in 1962–64, and as Population Council Regional Demographic Director for Africa in 1967–70 and with

Population Council support in Africa in 1970–71, 1972–73, and 1973–74 and in India and Bangladesh in 1977–78; with Australian National University support and in collaboration with the Population Centre, Bangalore, in India, for various periods, 1979–83; and with Ford Foundation support in Latin America, 1981; various periods in Egypt with support from the Cairo Demographic Centre.

202. October 1968 until February 1969, when with The Population Council, on an investigation designed with Parker Mauldin.

203. W. Parker Mauldin and Bernard Berelson, with Zenas Sykes, 'Conditions of fertility decline in developing countries,' *Studies in Family Planning*, 9(5), May 1978, pp. 89–147.

204. Cf. Benson R. Snyder, *The Hidden Curriculum*, Knopf, New York, 1971.

205. J. Gregory Williams, *Population Manpower in the Social Sciences*, PB-299518, National Institute for Child Health and Human Development, Washington, 1978, Table 7.32.

206. Review by John C. Caldwell of H. Yuan Tien (ed.), *Population Theory in China*, M. E. Sharpe, New York and Croom Helm, London, 1980, in *Journal of Conteporary Asia*, 12(4), 1982, pp. 506–8.

207. Cf. K. G. Basavarajappa and J. C. Caldwell, 'The employment and training in the ECAFE Region of persons with training in demography or allied population fields,' in *International Union for the Scientific Study of Population, Sydney Conference 21st to 25th August 1967, Contributed Papers* (Department of Demography, Australian National University, Canberra), pp. 1083–99.

208. John C. Caldwell and Barnett F. Baron, 'Technical Cooperation in demographic training and skill building,' paper presented at the Special Session on Technical Cooperation, IUSSP, Manila, 17 December 1981, Formal Group Discussion: F2.

209. Cf. Frank W. Notestein, 'Demography in the United States: A partial account of the development of the field,' *Population and Development Review*, 8(4), December 1982, pp. 651–87.

210. Dennis Hodgson, 'Demography as social science and policy science,' *Population and Development Review*, 9(1), March 1983, pp. 1–34. (The need to insert comment this late in the report arises from the fact that this issue of the journal did not reach Australia until June 1983.)

211. The Indianapolis Study which was designed in the period

180   *Notes*

1938-1940 and was in the field in 1941 is described as attempting to 'produce an explanation of the *postwar* (our italics) "baby boom".' The League of Nations work at OPR is described (p. 7) as beginning in 1936 when, in fact, 1941 is the correct date.

212. David Bell and Francis Sutton at the Lake Como Conference of 1967.
213. John C. Caldwell, 'The containment of world population growth,' *Studies in Family Planning,* 6(12), December 1975, pp. 429-36. (This paper was one of the opening addresses in the first session of the Tribune at the World Population Conference in Bucharest in 1974); United Nations Department of Economic and Social Affairs, *Concise Report on the World Population Situation in 1970-1975 and its Long-Range Implications,* Population Studies, No. 56, ST/ESA/Ser.A/56, United Nations, New York, 1974; United Nations, 1982, op. cit.
214. Amy O. Tsui and Donald J. Bogue, 'Declining world fertility: Trends, causes, implications,' *Population Bulletin,* 33(4), October 1978, Population Reference Bureau, Washington; Donald J. Bogue and Amy O. Tsui, 'Zeró world population growth?,' *Public Interest,* No. 55, Spring 1979, pp. 99-113.
215. Paul Demeny, 'On the end of the population explosion,' *Population and Development Review,* 5(1) March 1979, pp. 141-62; Donald J. Bogue and Amy O. Tsui, 'A reply to Paul Demeny's "On the end of the population explosion",' *Population and Development Review,* 5(3), September 1979, pp. 479-94; Paul Demeny, 'On the end of the population explosion: A rejoinder,' *Population and Development Review,* 5(3), September 1979, pp. 495-504.
216. United Nations, 1973, op. cit., p. 63; United Nations, 1982, op. cit.
217. John C. Caldwell, Graham E. Harrison, and Pat Quiggin, 'The demography of micro-states,' *World Development,* 8(12), December 1980, pp. 953-67.
218. United Nations, *Demographic Yearboook 1981*, United Nations, New York, 1981, p. 522.
219. Anrudh K. Jain and Arjun L. Adlakha, 'Preliminary estimates of fertility decline in India during the 1970s,' paper presented at the conference of the British Society for Population Studies, *India's Population*, Oxford, 14-16 December 1982.
220. The Sample Registration System recorded a crude birth-rate of

36.9 per thousand in 1971, falling to 33.0 in 1977, thereafter stabilizing or rising slightly to 33.2 in 1981 (India, Registrar General, Ministry of Home Affairs, *Sample Registration Bulletin*, 16(2), December 1982, p. 31).

221. Egypt recorded a crude birth-rate of 41 per thousand in 1966 when the National Family Planning Program began, falling to 34 in 1972, rising to 41 in 1979 and provisionally estimated as 38 in 1981 (United Nations, 1981, op. cit., pp. 518–19).

222. John C. Caldwell, P. H. Reddy, and Pat Caldwell, 'The causes of demographic change in rural South India: A micro approach,' *Population and Development Review*, 8(4), December 1982, pp. 689–727; Mead T. Cain, 'The economic activities of children in a village in Bangladesh,' *Population and Development Review*, 3(3), September 1977, pp. 201–27; Allan G. Hill, Sara C. Randall, and Oriel Sullivan, 'The mortality and fertility of farmers and pastoralists in central Mali 1950–1981,' *CPS Research Paper*, Nos. 82–4, May 1982, Centre for Population Studies, London School of Hygiene and Tropical Medicine.

223. Gunnar Myrdal, *An American Dilemma: The Negro Problem and Modern Democracy*, Harper and Brothers, New York, 1944.

224. Bernard Gilland, 'Considerations on world population and food supply,' *Population and Development Review*, 9(2), June 1983, pp. 203–11.

225. United Nations, 1982, op. cit., p. 58, with further calculations by Christine McLennan.

Index

education and training 45, 50, 92, 122
Fellowship Program 12, 44, 50, 55, 57, 102
funding of 34, 35, 47, 135, 142
mentioned 79, 99
Taichung Project 68, 69, 70
Population and Development Policy Research Program 127
Population Dynamics Program (US) 95
Population Dynamics Workshops 128
population growth 2-3, 8, 11-19, 21-4
and economic development 28-9, 134
in India 9-10, 13-14, 21-2, 29-43
in Third World countries 4, 10, 11, 33
research 34, 136
Population Institute, Bangkok 124
Population Investigation Committee (UK) 75
Population Policy Research Program *see* Population and Development Policy Research Program
Population Program (US) 52-3, 77, 78-81, 82-3, 134
population projections 5-6, 23, 29-30, 159-60
Population Reference Bureau 1
population research
ageing 123
birth rate 8, 128, 133
by governments 40-3, 98-105
contraception 6-7, 8, 18-19, 40
criticisms of 143-4
current trends 147-8, 159-60
epidemics 9
fertility 6, 7-8
Ford Foundation 4, 19, 31-6, 48-58, 59-76, 77-81, 88-9, 129-35
funding 1, 19, 32-3, 34-6, 90, 134-5
future of 129-35, 151-64
history of 4-30
impact of 139-42
mortality rate 4, 8, 15, 20, 23, 67, 133
political influences 33, 133-5
programs 54-8, 59-76, 104, 120-1, 123-4, 134-5, 143-50
Third World 1, 4, 10, 11, 19-30,

51, 57, 102, 106-26, 137-9, 143-50
Potharam Study of Family Planning Acceptability 124
Potter, R. 57, 124
Princeton University *see* Office of Population Research (US)
public health 1, 40, 89
history 82
programs 43, 82-97
public opinion
abortion 132, 133
brith control 18-19, 38, 39, 48-9, 52, 132-3, 139-40
Puerto Rico
birth control 77
population growth 21
population research 24, 34
University 34
Pullum, T. 107

Raina, B. L. 41, 42, 57
Rao, *Lady* R. 39
Ravenholt, R. 103, 134
religious opinion
birth control 48-9, 103, 105, 133-4, 138, 162
contraception 78, 106
reproductive biology *see* human reproduction
Revelle, R. 90
Rhodes Livingston Institute 162
Ridley, J. C. 55, 56
Right to Life Movement 132
Rizk, H. 111
Rock, J. 48
Rockefeller Foundation
and China 17
and Ford Foundation 126, 127
and India 42
and Third World countries, 13, 115, 155
birth control research 32, 99
demographic research 17
education and training 71, 86, 122
funding of 134
Khanna Project 57, 88, 124
public health research 17, 82
Williamsberg Conference 25, 32
Rockefeller, J. D. 3rd 17, 25, 32, 34, 36, 131
Memorial Fund 135
Rockefeller, N. 49